Date: 9/2/11

973.92 SOW
Sowell, Thomas,
Dismantling America :

DISMANTLING AMERICA

and other controversial essays

by THOMAS SOWELL

BASIC
BOOKS

A Member of the Perseus Books Group
New York

Copyright © 2010 by Thomas Sowell
Published by Basic Books,
A Member of the Perseus Books Group

All rights reserved. Printed in the United States of America.
No part of this book may be reproduced in any manner
whatsoever without written permission except in the
case of brief quotations embodied in critical articles and reviews.
For information, address Basic Books,
387 Park Avenue South, New York, NY 10016-8810.

Books published by Basic Books are available at special
discounts for bulk purchases in the United States by
corporations, institutions, and other organizations.
For more information, please contact the
Special Markets Department at the Perseus Books Group,
2300 Chestnut Street, Suite 200, Philadelphia, PA 19103,
or call (800) 810-4145, ext. 5000, or e-mail
special.markets@perseusbooks.com.

A CIP catalog record for this book is available
from the Library of Congress.

LCCN: 2010907169

ISBN: 978-0-465-02251-9

10 9 8 7 6 5 4 3 2 1

CONTENTS

Contents

PREFACE

There are Americans alive at this moment who may experience the national equivalent of "a perfect storm," either domestically or internationally, or both.

To have what is called "a perfect storm," many dangerous forces must come together at the same time. Those dangerous forces have been building in the United States of America for at least half a century. By 2010, increasing numbers of Americans were beginning to express fears that they were losing the country they grew up in, and that they had hoped— or perhaps too complacently *assumed*— that they would be passing on to their children and grandchildren.

No one issue and no one administration in Washington has been enough to create a perfect storm for a great nation that has weathered many storms in its more than two centuries of existence. But the Roman Empire lasted many times longer, and weathered many storms in its turbulent times— and yet it ultimately collapsed completely.

It has been estimated that a thousand years passed before the standard of living in Europe rose again to the level it had achieved in Roman times. The collapse of a civilization is not just the replacement of rulers or institutions with new rulers and new institutions. It is the destruction of a whole way of life and the painful, and sometimes pathetic, attempts to begin rebuilding amid the ruins.

Is that where America is headed? I believe it is. Our only saving grace is that we are not there yet— and that nothing is inevitable until it happens.

While the Obama administration in Washington is not the root cause of the ominous dangers that face this country, at home and abroad, it is the embodiment, the personification and the culmination of dangerous trends that began decades ago. Moreover, it has escalated those dangers to what may be a point of no return. The specifics of the missteps and the misdeeds of this administration are among the things chronicled, here and there, in the essays that follow, which were first published as my syndicated newspaper columns. But that such an administration could be elected in the first place, headed by a man whose only qualifications to be President of the United States at a dangerous time in the history of the world were rhetoric, style and symbolism— and whose animus against the values and institutions of America had been demonstrated repeatedly over a period of decades beforehand— speaks volumes about the inadequacies of our educational system and the degeneration of our culture.

That Barack Obama in office has often done the exact opposite of what Barack Obama said as a candidate, on issue after issue, should not cause half the surprise and disappointment that it has produced in many people who pinned high hopes on him.

The really painful surprise is that so many people based their hopes on his words, rather than on the record of his deeds. What that means is that, even if we somehow manage to survive this man's reckless economic policies at home and his potentially fatal foreign policy actions and inactions, the gullibility and fecklessness of those voters who put him in the White House will still be there to be exploited by the next master of glib demagoguery and emotional images, who can lead us into another vortex of dangers, from which there is no guarantee that we will emerge as a free people or even as a viable society.

Our concern is not with one man but with a country, though history has shown repeatedly that one man in a key position at a crucial time can bring down a whole country in ruins. But history is just one of the things whose neglect has contributed toward the confluence of forces that can produce a perfect storm. When we look back at the decades-long erosions and distortions of our educational system, our legal system and our political system, we must acknowledge the chilling fact that the kinds of dangers we face now were always inherent in these degenerating trends. The essays that follow deal with these trends individually, but it may help to keep in mind that they were all going on at the same time, and that these are the dangers whose coming together can create a perfect storm.

GOVERNMENT POLICIES

Government policies can be judged by what they promise or by what they do. While it might seem to be obvious that the latter is what is relevant, many people nevertheless assume that rent control laws control rent, gun control laws control guns, stimulus spending stimulates the economy and jobs bills create jobs. Moreover, few people seem to find it necessary to check any of these assumptions against facts. For example, the fact that cities like New York and San Francisco, with a long history of very strong rent control laws, have some of the highest rents in the country might suggest that such assumptions need a lot closer attention than either the public or the media give them.

People who say that the government has to "do something" when there is an economic downturn almost never compare what actually happened when the government did something, as in the wake of the 1929 stock market crash, compared to what happened when the government did nothing after a comparable stock market crash in 1987— or in fact after a number of other crashes before 1929. Facts seem to have become irrelevant, for all too many people, who rely instead on visions and rhetoric.

The same reliance on familiar words, rather than on demonstrable facts, applies even to international relations, including life-and-death issues of national security. Thus people who advocate disarmament agreements are automatically called "the peace movement," without any recourse to the history of the actual outcomes of disarmament agreements, which flourished as perhaps never before, between the two World Wars. These agreements disarmed the Western democracies, both literally and figuratively, making them more vulnerable to the aggressive dictatorships that were free to violate disarmament agreements with impunity. The net result was that one-sided disarmament made war look more winnable to the Axis powers and therefore made war more attractive, despite the rhetoric of the so-called "peace movement."

Separating words from realities is one of the most important steps toward evaluating government policies, whether domestically or internationally. Since rhetorical skills are among the most highly developed skills among politicians, any serious attempt to see government policies for what they are means keeping our eyes fixed on facts, despite the distractions of rhetoric. The essays that follow seek to bring out some of those facts. More important, they seek to penetrate the fog of rhetoric.

Dismantling America

Just one year ago, would you have believed that an unelected government official, not even a Cabinet member confirmed by the Senate but simply one of the many "czars" appointed by the President, could arbitrarily cut the pay of executives in private businesses by 50 percent or 90 percent?

Did you think that another "czar" would be talking about restricting talk radio? That there would be plans afloat to subsidize newspapers— that is, to create a situation where some newspapers' survival would depend on the government liking what they publish?

Did you imagine that anyone would even be talking about having a panel of so-called "experts" deciding who could and could not get life-saving medical treatments?

Scary as that is from a medical standpoint, it is also chilling from the standpoint of freedom. If you have a mother who needs a heart operation or a child with some dire medical condition, how free would you feel to speak out against an administration that has the power to make life and death decisions about your loved ones?

Does any of this sound like America?

How about a federal agency giving school children material to enlist them on the side of the president? Merely being assigned to sing his praises in class is apparently not enough.

How much of America would be left if the federal government continued on this path? President Obama has already floated the idea of a national police force, something we have done without for more than two centuries.

We already have local police forces all across the country and military forces for national defense, as well as the FBI for federal crimes and the National Guard for local emergencies. What would be the role of a national police force created by Barack Obama, with all its leaders appointed by him? It would seem more like the brown shirts of dictators than like anything American.

How far the President will go depends of course on how much resistance he meets. But the direction in which he is trying to go tells us more than all his rhetoric or media spin.

Barack Obama has not only said that he is out to "change the United States of America," the people he has been associated with for years have expressed in words and deeds their hostility to the values, the principles and the people of this country.

Jeremiah Wright said it with words: "God damn America!" Bill Ayers said it with the bombs that he planted. Community activist goons have said it with their contempt for the rights of other people.

Among the people appointed as czars by President Obama have been people who have praised enemy dictators like Mao, or who have seen the public schools as places to promote sexual practices contrary to the values of most Americans, to a captive audience of children.

Those who say that the Obama administration should have investigated those people more thoroughly before appointing them are missing the point completely. Why should we assume that Barack Obama didn't know what such people were like, when he has been associating with precisely these kinds of people for decades before he reached the White House?

Nothing is more consistent with his lifelong patterns than putting such people in government— people who reject American values, resent Americans in general and successful Americans in particular, as well as resenting America's influence in the world.

Any miscalculation on his part would be in not thinking that others would discover what these stealth appointees were like. Had it not been for the Fox News Channel, these stealth appointees might have remained unexposed for what they are. Fox News is now high on the administration's enemies list.

Nothing so epitomizes President Obama's own contempt for American values and traditions like ramming two bills through Congress in his first year— each bill more than a thousand pages long— too fast for either of them to be read, much less discussed. Some people are starting to wake up. Whether enough people will wake up in time to keep America from being dismantled, piece by piece, is another question— and the biggest question for this generation.

Dismantling America: Part II

M any years ago, at a certain academic institution, there was an experimental program that the faculty had to vote on as to whether or not it should be made permanent.

I rose at the faculty meeting to say that I knew practically nothing about whether the program was good or bad, and that the information that had been supplied to us was too vague for us to have any basis for voting, one way or the other. My suggestion was that we get more concrete information before having a vote.

The director of that program rose immediately and responded indignantly and sarcastically to what I had just said— and the faculty gave him a standing ovation.

After the faculty meeting was over, I told a colleague that I was stunned and baffled by the faculty's fierce response to my simply saying that we needed more information before voting.

"Tom, you don't understand," he said. "Those people need to believe in that man. They have invested so much hope and trust in him that they cannot let you stir up any doubts."

Years later, and hundreds of miles away, I learned that my worst misgivings about that program did not begin to approach the reality, which included organized criminal activity.

The memory of that long-ago episode has come back more than once, while observing both the actions of the

Obama administration and the fierce reactions of its supporters to any questioning or criticism.

Almost never do these reactions include factual or logical arguments against the administration's critics. Instead, there is indignation, accusations of bad faith and even charges of racism.

Here too, it seems as if so many people have invested so much hope and trust in Barack Obama that it is intolerable that anyone should come along and stir up any doubts that could threaten their house of cards.

Among the most pathetic letters and e-mails I receive are those from people who ask why I don't write more "positively" about Obama or "give him the benefit of the doubt."

No one— not even the President of the United States— has an entitlement to a "positive" response to his actions. The entitlement mentality has eroded the once common belief that you earned things, including respect, instead of being given them.

As for the benefit of the doubt, no one— *especially* not the President of the United States— is entitled to that, when his actions can jeopardize the rights of 300 million Americans domestically and the security of the nation in an international jungle, where nuclear weapons may soon be in the hands of people with suicidal fanaticism. Will it take a mushroom cloud over an American city to make that clear? Was 9/11 not enough?

When a President of the United States has begun the process of dismantling America from within, and exposing us to dangerous enemies outside, the time is long past for being concerned about his public image. He has his own press agents for that.

Internationally, Barack Obama has made every mistake that was made by the Western democracies in the 1930s, mistakes that put Hitler in a position to start World War II— and come dangerously close to winning it.

At the heart of those mistakes was trying to mollify your enemies by throwing your friends to the wolves. The Obama administration has already done that by reneging on this country's commitment to put a missile defense shield in Eastern Europe and by its lackadaisical foot-dragging on doing anything serious to stop Iran from getting nuclear weapons. That means, for all practical purposes, throwing Israel to the wolves as well.

Countries around the world that have to look out for their own national survival, above all, are not going to ignore how much Obama has downgraded the reliability of America's commitments.

Iraq, for example, knows that Iran is going to be next door forever, while Americans may be gone in a few years. South Korea likewise knows that North Korea is permanently next door but who knows when the Obama administration will get a bright idea to pull out? Countries in South America know that Hugo Chavez is allying Venezuela with Iran. Dare they ally themselves with an unreliable U.S.A.? Or should they join our enemies to work against us?

This issue is too serious for squeamish silence.

Playing Freedom Cheap

I f eternal vigilance is the price of freedom, incessant distractions are the way that politicians take away our freedoms, in order to enhance their own power and longevity in office. Dire alarms and heady crusades are among the many distractions of our attention from the ever increasing ways that government finds to take away more of our money and more of our freedom.

Magicians have long known that distracting an audience is the key to creating the illusion of magic. It is also the key to political magic.

Alarms ranging from "overpopulation" to "global warming" and crusades ranging from "affordable housing" to "universal health care" have been among the distractions of political magicians. But few distractions have had such a long and impressive political track record as getting people to resent and, if necessary, hate other people.

The most politically effective totalitarian systems have gotten people to give up their own freedom in order to vent their resentment or hatred at other people— under Communism, the capitalists; under Nazis, the Jews.

Under extremist Islamic regimes today, hatred is directed at the infidels in general and the "great Satan," the United States, in particular. There, some people have been induced to give up not only their freedom but even their lives, in order to strike a blow against those they have been taught to hate.

We have not yet reached these levels of hostility, but those who are taking away our freedoms, bit by bit, on the installment plan, have been incessantly supplying us with people to resent.

One of the most audacious attempts to take away our freedom to live our lives as we see fit has been the so-called "health care reform" bills that were being rushed through Congress before either the public or the members of Congress themselves had a chance to discover all that was in them.

For this, we were taught to resent doctors, insurance companies and even people with "Cadillac health insurance plans," who were to be singled out for special taxes. Meanwhile, our freedom to make our own medical decisions— on which life and death can depend— was to be quietly taken from us and transferred to our betters in Washington.

Another dangerous power toward which we are moving, bit by bit, on the installment plan, is the power of politicians to tell people what their incomes can and cannot be. Here the resentment is being directed against "the rich."

The distracting phrases here include "obscene" wealth and "unconscionable" profits. But, if we stop and think about it— which politicians don't expect us to— what is obscene about wealth? Wouldn't we consider it great if every human being on earth had a billion dollars and lived in a place that could rival the Taj Mahal?

Poverty is obscene. It is poverty that needs to be reduced— and increasing a country's productivity has done that far more widely than redistributing income by targeting "the rich."

You can see the agenda behind the rhetoric when profits are called "unconscionable" but taxes never are, even when taxes take more than half of what someone has earned, or add much more to the prices we have to pay than profits do.

The assumption that what *A* pays *B* is any business of *C* is an assumption that means a dangerous power being transferred to politicians to tell us all what incomes we can and cannot receive. It will not apply to everyone all at once. Like the income tax, which at first applied only to the truly rich, and then slowly but steadily moved down the income scale to hit the rest of us, the power to say what incomes people can be allowed to make will inevitably move down the income scale to make us all dependents and supplicants of politicians.

The phrase "public servants" is increasingly misleading. They are well on their way to becoming public masters— like aptly named White House "czars." The more they can get us all to resent those they designate, the more they can distract us from their increasing control of our own lives— but only if we sell our freedom cheap. We can sell our birthright and not even get the mess of pottage.

Pretty Talk and Ugly Realities

No phrase represents more of a triumph of hope over experience than the phrase "Middle East peace process." A close second might be the once-fashionable notion that Israel should "trade land for peace."

Since everybody seems to be criticizing Israel for its military response to the rockets being fired into their country from the Gaza Strip, let me add my criticisms as well. The Israelis traded land for peace, but they have never gotten the peace, so they should take back the land.

Maybe a couple of generations of Palestinians in Gaza living in peace under Israeli occupation and a couple of generations of the occupation troops squelching the terrorists— "militants" for those of you who are squeamish— would set up conditions where the Palestinians would be free to vote on whether they would like to remain occupied or to have their own state— minus terrorists and their rockets.

Casualty totals alone should be enough to show that the Palestinian people are the biggest losers from the current situation, where the terrorists among them, firing rockets into Israel, can bring devastating retaliatory strikes.

Why don't the Palestinians vote for some representatives who would make a lasting peace with

Israel? Because any such candidates would be killed by the terrorists long before election day, so nobody volunteers for that dangerous role.

We don't know what the Palestinians really want—and won't know as long as they are ruled by Hamas, Hezbollah and the like.

Whatever the benefits of peace for the Palestinian population, what are the terrorists going to do in peacetime? Become librarians and furniture salesmen?

So-called "world opinion" has been a largely negative factor in this situation. Nothing is easier than for people living in peace and safety in Paris or Rome to call for a "cease fire" after the Israelis retaliate against people who are firing rockets into their country.

The time to cease fire was before the rockets were fired.

What do calls for "cease fire" and "negotiations" do? They lower the price of launching attacks. This is true not only in the Middle East but in other parts of the world as well.

During the Vietnam war, when American clergymen were crying out "Stop the bombing!" they paid little attention to the fact that bombing pauses made it easier for North Vietnam to move more ammunition into South Vietnam to kill both South Vietnamese and Americans.

After Argentina invaded the Falkland Islands, if British Prime Minister Margaret Thatcher had heeded calls for a "cease fire," that would have simply lowered the price to be paid by the Argentine government for their invasion.

Go back a hundred years— before there was a United Nations and before "world opinion" was taken into account.

An Argentine invasion of the Falkland Islands at that time would have risked not only a British counterattack to retake the islands but also British attacks on Argentina itself.

Anywhere in the world, attacks such as those on Israel today would not only have risked retaliation but invasion and annihilation of the government that launched those attacks.

Today, so-called "world opinion" not only limits the price to be paid for aggression or terrorism, it has even led to the self-indulgence of third parties talking pretty talk about limiting the response of those who are attacked to what is "proportionate."

By this reasoning, we should not have declared war on Japan for bombing Pearl Harbor. We should have gone over to Japan, bombed one of their harbors— and let it go at that.

Does anyone imagine that this would have led to Japan's becoming as peaceful today as it has become after Hiroshima and Nagasaki?

Or is the real agenda to engage in moral preening from a safe distance and at somebody else's expense?

Those who think "negotiations" are a magic answer seem not to understand that when *A* wants to annihilate *B*, this is not an "issue" that can be resolved amicably around a conference table.

The Blame Game

After virtually every disaster created by Beltway politicians you can hear the sound of feet scurrying for cover in Washington, see fingers pointing in every direction away from Washington, and watch all sorts of scapegoats hauled up before Congressional committees to be denounced on television for the disasters created by members of the committee who are lecturing them.

The word repeated endlessly in these political charades is "deregulation." The idea is that it was a lack of government supervision which allowed "greed" in the private sector to lead the nation into crises that only our Beltway saviors can solve.

What utter rubbish this all is can be found by checking the record of how government regulators were precisely the ones who imposed lower mortgage lending standards— and it was members of Congress (of both parties) who pushed the regulators, the banks and the mortgage-buying giants Fannie Mae and Freddie Mac into accepting risky mortgages, in the name of "affordable housing" and more home ownership. Presidents of both parties also jumped on the bandwagon.

Most people don't have time to spend digging into the *Congressional Record* and other sources to find out the ugly truth being covered up by the blizzard of lies coming out of Washington and echoed in much of the media. But my research assistants do that for a living, and it is all presented in a book of mine titled *The Housing Boom and Bust.*

When the housing boom was going along merrily, Congressman Barney Frank was proud to be one of those who were pushing Fannie Mae and Freddie Mac into more adventurous financial practices, in the name of "affordable housing."

In 2003 he said: "I believe that we, as the Federal Government, have probably done too little rather than too much to push them to meet the goals of affordable housing and to set reasonable goals." He added: "I want to roll the dice a little bit more in this situation towards subsidized housing."

In other words, when things were looking good, he was happy to acknowledge the role of the federal government in pushing the housing market in a direction it would not have taken on its own. But, after the risky mortgage-lending practices fostered by government intervention led to massive defaults and foreclosures that caused financial institutions to collapse or be bailed out, Congressman Frank changed his tune completely.

By 2007, his line was now that "the subprime crisis demonstrates the serious negative economic and social consequences that result from too little regulation." By 2008, his line was that the financial crisis was caused by "bad decisions that were made by people in the private sector."

When television financial reporter Maria Bartiromo reminded Congressman Frank of his statements in earlier years, he simply denied making the statements she quoted and blamed "right-wing Republicans who took the position that regulation was always bad."

Regulation is of course not always bad, and it would be hard to find anyone of any party who says that it is. Moreover, Congressman Frank had some Republican collaborators in pushing regulators to push banks into risky mortgage lending.

As for the market, financial market specialist Mark Zandi put it very plainly: "Lending money to American homebuyers had been one of the least risky and most profitable businesses a bank could engage in for nearly a century."

What changed that was not the market but politicians like Barney Frank and his Senate counterpart Christopher Dodd, pushing the "affordable housing" crusade through government intervention, in disregard of the risks that they were repeatedly warned about by people inside and outside of government.

Although this is the biggest housing disaster the government has ever produced, it is by no means the first. Republicans intervened in the housing markets to promote more home ownership in the 1920s, Democrats in the 1930s and both parties after World War II. All of these interventions led to massive foreclosures.

Don't politicians ever learn? Why should they? What they have learned all too well is how easy it is to get credit for promoting home ownership and how easy it is to escape blame for the later foreclosures and other economic disasters that follow.

Bowing to "World Opinion"

I n the string of amazing decisions made during the first year of the Obama administration, nothing seems more like sheer insanity than the decision to try foreign terrorists, who have committed acts of war against the United States, in federal court, as if they were American citizens accused of crimes.

Terrorists are not even entitled to the protection of the Geneva Convention, much less the Constitution of the United States. Terrorists have never observed, nor even claimed to have observed, the Geneva Convention, nor are they among those covered by it.

But over and above the utter inconsistency of what is being done is the utter recklessness it represents. The last time an attack on the World Trade Center was treated as a matter of domestic criminal justice was after a bomb was exploded there in 1993. Under the rules of American criminal law, the prosecution had to turn over all sorts of information to the defense—information that told the Al Qaeda international terrorist network what we knew about them and how we knew it.

This was nothing more and nothing less than giving away military secrets to an enemy in wartime—something for which people have been executed, as they should have been. Secrecy in warfare is a matter of life and death. Lives were risked and lost during World War II to prevent Nazi Germany from discovering that

Britain had broken its supposedly unbreakable Enigma code and could read their military plans that were being radioed in that code.

"Loose lips sink ships" was the World War II motto in the United States. But loose lips are mandated under the rules of criminal prosecutions.

Tragically, this administration seems hell-bent to avoid seeing acts of terrorism against the United States as acts of war. The very phrase "war on terrorism" is avoided, as if that will stop the terrorists' war on us.

The mindset of the left behind such thinking was spelled out in an editorial in the *San Francisco Chronicle*, which said that "Khalid Shaikh Mohammed, the professed mastermind of the 9/11 terrorist attacks, will be tried the right way— the American way, in a federal courtroom where the world will see both his guilt and the nation's adherence to the rule of law."

This is not the rule of law but the application of laws to situations for which they were not designed.

How many Americans may pay with their lives for the intelligence secrets and methods that can be forced to be disclosed to Al Qaeda was not mentioned. Nor was there mention of how many foreign nations and individuals whose cooperation with us in the war on terror have been involved in countering Al Qaeda— nor how many foreign nations and individuals will have to think twice now, before cooperating with us again, when their role can be revealed in court to our enemies, who can exact revenge on them.

Behind this decision and others is the notion that we have to demonstrate our good faith to other nations, sometimes called "world opinion." Just who are these saintly nations whose favor we must curry, at the risk of American lives and the national security of the United States?

Internationally, the law of the jungle ultimately prevails, despite pious talk about "the international community" and "world opinion," or the pompous and corrupt farce of the United Nations. Yet this is the gallery to which Barack Obama has been playing, both before and after becoming President of the United States.

In the wake of the obscenity of a trial of terrorists in federal court for an act of war— and the worldwide propaganda platform it will give them— it may seem to be a small thing that President Obama has been photographed yet again bowing deeply to a foreign ruler. But how large or small an act is depends on its actual consequences, not on whether the politically correct intelligentsia think it is no big deal.

As a private citizen, Barack Obama has a right to make as big a jackass of himself as he wants to. But, as President of the United States, his actions not only denigrate a nation that other nations rely on for survival, but raise questions about how reliable our judgment and resolve are— which in turn raises questions about whether those nations will consider themselves better off to make the best deal they can with our enemies.

Subsidizing Bad Decisions

Now that the federal government has decided to bail out homeowners in trouble, with mortgage loans up to $729,000, that raises some questions that ought to be asked, but are seldom being asked.

Since the average American never took out a mortgage loan as big as seven hundred grand— for the very good reason that he could not afford it— why should he be forced as a taxpayer to subsidize someone else who apparently couldn't afford it either, but who got in over his head anyway?

Why should taxpayers who live in apartments, perhaps because they did not feel that they could afford to buy a house, be forced to subsidize other people who could not afford to buy a house, but who went ahead and bought one anyway?

We hear a lot of talk in some quarters about how any one of us could be in the same financial trouble that many homeowners are in if we lost our job or had some other misfortune. The pat phrase is that we are all just a few paydays away from being in the same predicament.

Another way of saying the same thing is that some people live high enough on the hog that any of the common misfortunes of life can ruin them.

Who hasn't been out of work at some time or other, or had an illness or accident that created unexpected expenses? The old and trite notion of "saving for a rainy day" is old and trite precisely because this has been a common experience for a very long time.

What is new is the current notion of indulging people who refused to save for a rainy day or to live within their means. In politics, it is called "compassion"— which comes in both the standard liberal version and "compassionate conservatism."

The one person toward whom there is no compassion is the taxpayer.

The current political stampede to stop mortgage foreclosures proceeds as if foreclosures are just something that strikes people like a bolt of lightning from the blue— and as if the people facing foreclosures are the only people that matter.

What if the foreclosures are not stopped?

Will millions of homes just sit empty? Or will new people move into those homes, now selling for lower prices— prices perhaps more within the means of the new occupants?

The same politicians who have been talking about a need for "affordable housing" for years are now suddenly alarmed that home prices are falling. How can housing become more affordable unless prices fall?

The political meaning of "affordable housing" is housing that is made more affordable by politicians intervening to create government subsidies, rent control or other gimmicks for which politicians can take credit.

Affordable housing produced by market forces provides no benefit to politicians and has no attraction for them.

Study after study, not only here but in other countries, show that the most affordable housing is where there has been the least government interference with the market— contrary to rhetoric.

When new occupants of foreclosed housing find it more affordable, will the previous occupants all become homeless? Or are they more likely to move into homes or apartments that they can afford? They will of course be sadder— but perhaps wiser as well.

The old and trite phrase "sadder but wiser" is old and trite for the same reason that "saving for a rainy day" is old and trite. It reflects an all too common human experience.

Even in an era of much-ballyhooed "change," the government cannot eliminate sadness. What it can do is transfer that sadness from those who made risky and unwise decisions to the taxpayers who had nothing to do with their decisions.

Worse, the subsidizing of bad decisions destroys one of the most effective sources of better decisions— namely, paying the consequences of bad decisions.

In the wake of the housing debacle in California, more people are buying less expensive homes, making bigger down payments, and staying away from "creative" and risky financing. It is amazing how fast people learn when they are not insulated from the consequences of their decisions.

Are You an "Extremist"?

While the rest of us may be worried about violent Mexican drug gangs on our border, or about terrorists who are going to be released from Guantanamo, the Director of Homeland Security is worried about "right-wing extremists."

Just who are these right-wing extremists?

According to an official document of the U.S. Department of Homeland Security, right-wing extremists include "groups and individuals that are dedicated to a single issue, such as opposition to abortion or immigration." It also includes those "rejecting federal authority in favor of state or local authority."

If you fit into any of these categories, you may not have realized that you are considered a threat to national security. But apparently the Obama administration has its eye on you.

According to the same official document, the Department of Homeland Security "has no specific information that domestic rightwing terrorists are currently planning acts of violence." But somehow they just know that you right-wingers are itching to unleash terror somewhere, somehow.

So-called "honor killings" by Muslims in the United States, including a recent beheading of his wife by a leader of one of the American Muslim organizations, do not seem to arouse any concern by the Department of Homeland Security.

When it comes to the thuggery of community activist groups— their members harassing the homes of bankers and even the home of Senator Phil Gramm when he opposed things that these community activist groups favored— the Department of Homeland Security apparently sees no evil, hears no evil and speaks no evil.

Maybe they are too busy worrying about right-wing "extremists" who don't like abortions or illegal immigration, or who favor the division of power between the state and federal governments established by the Constitution.

In one sense, the Department of Homeland Security paper is silly. In another sense, it can be sinister as a revealing and disturbing sign of the preoccupations and priorities of this administration— and their willingness to witch hunt and demonize those who dare to disagree with them.

Reportedly, the FBI and the Defense Department are cooperating with the Department of Homeland Security in investigations of returning veterans from Iraq and Afghanistan. That people who have put their lives on the line for this country are made the target of what is called the Vigilant Eagle program suggests that this administration might be more of a threat than the people they are investigating.

All this activity takes on a more sinister aspect against the background of one of the statements of Barack Obama during last year's election campaign that got remarkably little attention in the media. He suggested the creation of a federal police force, comparable in size to the military.

Why such an organization? For what purpose?

Since there are state and local police forces all across the country, an FBI to investigate federal crimes and a Department of Justice to prosecute those who commit them, as well as a Defense Department with military forces, just what role would a federal police force play?

Maybe it was just one of those bright ideas that gets floated during an election campaign. Yet there was no grassroots demand for any such federal police force nor any media clamor for it, so there was not even any political reason to suggest such a thing.

What would be different about a new federal police force, as compared to existing law enforcement and military forces? It would be a creation of the Obama administration, run by people appointed from top to bottom by that administration— and without the conflicting loyalties of those steeped in existing military traditions and law enforcement traditions.

In short, a federal police force could become President Obama's personal domestic political army, his own storm troopers.

Perhaps there will never be such a federal police force. But the targeting of individuals and groups who believe in some of the fundamental values on which this country was founded, and people who have demonstrated their patriotism by volunteering for military service, suggests that this potential for political abuse is worth watching, as Obama tries to remake America to fit his vision.

Varieties of Nothing

Doing nothing might seem to be simple and easy. But there are many varieties of nothing, and some kinds of nothing can get very elaborate and complex.

In courts of law, for example, "concurrent sentences" mean that nothing is being done to punish a convicted criminal for some of his crimes, since the time he is serving for one crime is being served concurrently with the time served for other crimes.

A study in Britain found that, among criminals caught, convicted and sentenced, only 7 percent of these sentences involved being put behind bars. Most of what is done in the other 93 percent of the cases amounts to virtually nothing.

People convicted of burglary in Britain are seldom jailed. For this and many other crimes, they will get a stern talking to. And, if they do it again, they will get an even sterner talking to.

The idea is that burglary is "only" a property crime and the left intelligentsia in Britain show their disdain for property rights by not taking property crimes very seriously. The net result is that burglary is far more common in Britain than in the United States.

Moreover, burglars in Britain seldom bother to "case" the place as most American burglars do before breaking in. Even if someone is home, that is far less of a danger in Britain where severe gun control laws greatly reduce the dangers to burglars.

A British homeowner who held two burglars at gunpoint until the police arrived was arrested— even though the gun he used turned out to be just a realistic-looking toy gun. The British intelligentsia take guns much more seriously than they take burglary, even when it is only a toy gun that is used to "intimidate" a burglar, as they put it.

People who say that we should learn from other countries seem to have in mind that we should imitate those countries. But some of the most valuable lessons from other countries can be had from seeing the disasters their policies have produced— especially when our own intelligentsia are pushing ideas that have already been tried and failed elsewhere.

We need to pay attention to these sneak previews of coming attractions, even if they consist of doing nothing. Whether in the United States or in other countries, the purpose of all this nothing is of course to pacify public opinion by pretending to be doing something.

The criminal justice system is not the only arena in which doing nothing is often common— and often gets complicated. On the international stage, the great arena for doing nothing is the United Nations.

We have, for example, been doing nothing to stop Iran from getting nuclear bombs, but it has been elaborate, multifaceted and complexly nuanced nothing.

Had there been no United Nations, it would have been obvious to all and sundry that we were doing nothing— and that could have had dire political consequences at election time.

However, thanks to the United Nations, there is a place where political leaders can go to do nothing, with a flurry of highly visible activity— and the media will cover it in detail, with a straight face, so that people will think that something is actually being done.

There may be televised statements and counter-statements— passionate debate among people wearing exotic apparel from different nations, all in an impressive, photogenic setting. U.N. resolutions may be voted upon and published to the world. It can be some of the best nothing that money can buy.

Even when United Nations resolutions contain lofty and ringing phrases about the "concerns" of "the international community" or invoke "world opinion"— or perhaps even warn of "grave consequences"— none of this is likely to lead any country to do anything that it would not have done otherwise.

Iran, for example, has for years ignored repeated U.N. resolutions and warnings against building nuclear facilities that can produce bombs. There is not the slightest reason to believe that they will stop unless they get stopped.

Certainly doing nothing will not stop them— not even elaborate diplomatic nothing or even presidential international speech-making nothing.

What Are They Buying?

Everyone is talking about how much money the government is spending, but very little attention is being paid to where they are spending it or what they are buying with it.

The government is putting money into banks, even when the banks don't want it, in hopes that the banks will put it into circulation. But the latest statistics show that banks are lending even less money now than they were before the government dumped all that cash on them.

Even if it had worked, putting cash into banks, in hopes that they would put it into circulation, seems a rather roundabout way of doing things, especially when the staggering sums of money involved are being justified as an "emergency" measure.

Spending money for infrastructure is another time-consuming way of dealing with what is called an immediate crisis. Infrastructure takes forever to plan, debate, and go through all sorts of hearings and adjudications, before getting approval to build from all the regulatory agencies involved.

Out of $355 billion newly appropriated, the Congressional Budget Office estimates that only $26 billion will be spent this fiscal year and only $110 billion by the end of next year.

Using long, drawn-out processes to put money into circulation to meet an emergency is like mailing a letter to the fire department to tell them that your house is on fire.

If you cut taxes tomorrow, people would have more money in their next paycheck, and it would probably be spent by the time they got that paycheck, through increased credit card purchases beforehand.

If all this sound and fury in Washington was about getting an economic crisis behind us, tax cuts could do that a lot faster.

None of this is rocket science. And Washington politicians are not all crazy, even if sometimes it looks that way. Often, what they say makes no sense because what they claim to be doing is not what they are actually doing.

No matter how many times President Barack Obama tells us that these "extraordinary times" call for "swift action," the kind of economic policies he is promoting take effect very slowly, no matter how quickly the legislation is rushed through Congress. It is the old Army game of hurry up and wait.

If the Beltway politicians aren't really trying to solve this crisis as quickly as they could, what are they trying to do?

One important clue may be a recent statement by President Obama's chief of staff, Rahm Emanuel, that "A crisis is a terrible thing to waste."

This is the kind of cynical revelation that sometimes slips out, despite all the political pieties and spin. Crises have long been seen as great opportunities to expand the federal government's power while the people are too scared to object and before any opposition can get organized.

That is why there is such haste to do things that will take effect slowly.

What are the Beltway politicians buying with all the hundreds of billions of dollars they are spending? They are buying what politicians are most interested in— power.

In the name of protecting the taxpayers' investment, they are buying the power to tell General Motors how to make cars, banks how to bank and, before it is all over with, all sorts of other people how to do the work they specialize in, and for which members of Congress have no competence, much less expertise.

This administration and Congress are now in a position to do what Franklin D. Roosevelt did during the Great Depression of the 1930s— use a crisis of the times to create new institutions that will last for generations.

To this day, we are still subsidizing millionaires in agriculture because farmers were having a tough time in the 1930s. We have the Federal National Mortgage Association ("Fannie Mae") taking reckless chances in the housing market that have blown up in our faces today, because FDR decided to create a new federal housing agency in 1938.

Who knows what bright ideas this administration will turn into permanent institutions for our children and grandchildren to try to cope with?

Cheap Political Theater

Death threats to executives at AIG, because of the bonuses they received, are one more sign of the utter degeneration of politics in our time.

Congressman Barney Frank has threatened to summon these executives before his committee and force them to reveal their home addresses— which would of course put their wives and children at the mercy of whatever kooks might want to literally take a shot at them.

Whatever the political or economic issues involved, this is not the way such issues should be resolved in America. We are not yet a banana republic, though that is the direction in which some of our politicians are taking us— especially those politicians who make a lot of noise about "compassion" and "social justice."

What makes this all the more painfully ironic is that it is precisely those members of Congress who have had the most to do with creating the risks that led to the current economic crisis who are making the most noise against others, and summoning people before their committee to be browbeaten and humiliated on nationwide television.

No one pushed harder than Congressman Barney Frank to force banks and other financial institutions to reduce their mortgage lending standards, in order to meet government-set goals for more home ownership. Those lower mortgage lending standards are at the heart of the increased riskiness of the mortgage market and of the collapse of Wall Street securities based on those risky mortgages.

Senator Christopher Dodd has played the same role in the Senate as Barney Frank played in the House of Representatives. Now both are summoning government employees and the officials of financial institutions before their committees to be lambasted in front of the media.

Dodd and Frank know that the best defense is a good offense. Both know how hard it would be to defend their own roles in the housing debacle, so they go on the offensive against others who are in no position to reply in kind, given the vindictive powers of Congress.

This political theater is in one sense cheap beyond words. In another sense, it is costly beyond words.

It is cheap because the politicians who are creating this distraction from their own role also voted for the very legislation that enabled contracted bonuses to be paid by companies like AIG that received government bailout money. If members of Congress can't be bothered to read the laws they pass, then they have no basis for whipping up lynch mob outrage against people who did read the law and acted within the law.

Just as everyone seemed to be a military expert a couple of years ago, when it was chic to say that the "surge" in Iraq would not work, so today everyone seems to be an expert on executive pay.

Whether the particular executives who received bonuses were the ones responsible for AIG's problems, or were among those who warned against those problems, is something that those of us on the outside don't know. That includes those in politics and the media who are making the loudest noise.

The politicians claim to be protecting the taxpayers' money. But having politicians trying to micro-manage any business is far more likely to make those businesses lose more money, including the taxpayers' money.

Securities based on risky mortgages are what toppled financial institutions but it was the government that made the mortgages risky in the first place, by making home-ownership statistics the holy grail, for which everything else was to be sacrificed, including commonsense standards for making home loans.

Politicians and bureaucrats micro-managing the mortgage sector of the economy is precisely how today's economic disaster began. Why anyone would think that their micro-managing the automobile industry, or executive pay across a wide sweep of other industries, is likely to make things better in the economy is a mystery.

The real point is to pander to envy and resentment against people who make a lot of money. Envy is always referred to by its political alias, "social justice." But to put the lives of the wives and children of executives at risk for the sake of Beltway grandstanding shows how low our political saviors have sunk.

The Limits of Power

When I first began to study the history of slavery around the world, many years ago, one of the oddities that puzzled me was the practice of paying certain slaves, which existed in ancient Rome and in America's antebellum South, among other places.

In both Rome and the South, slaveowners or their overseers whipped slaves to force them to work, and in neither place was whipping a slave literally to death likely to bring any serious consequences.

There could hardly be a greater power of one human being over another than the arbitrary power of life and death. Why then was it necessary to pay certain slaves? At the very least, it suggested that there were limits to what could be accomplished by power.

Most slaves performing most tasks were of course not paid, but were simply forced to work by the threat of punishment. That was sufficient for galley slaves or plantation slaves. But there were various kinds of work where that was not sufficient.

Tasks involving judgment or talents were different because no one can know how much judgment or talent someone else has. In short, knowledge is an inherent constraint on power. Payment can bring forth the knowledge or talent by giving those who have it an incentive to reveal it and to develop it.

Payment can vary in amount and in kind. Some slaves, especially eunuchs in the days of the Ottoman

Empire, could amass both wealth and power. One reason they could be trusted in positions of power was that they had no incentive to betray the existing rulers and try to establish their own dynasties, which would obviously have been physically impossible for them.

At more mundane levels, such tasks as diving operations in the Carolina swamps required a level of discretion and skill far in excess of that required to pick cotton in the South or cut sugar cane in the tropics. Slaves diving in the Carolina swamps had financial incentives and were treated far better. So were slaves working in Virginia's tobacco factories.

The point of all this is that when even slaves had to be paid to get certain kinds of work done, this shows the limits of what can be accomplished by power alone. Yet so much of what is said and done by those who rely on the power of government to direct ever more sweeping areas of our life seem to have no sense of the limits of what can be accomplished that way.

Even the totalitarian governments of the 20th century eventually learned the hard way the limits of what could be accomplished by power alone. China still has a totalitarian government today but, after the death of Mao, the Chinese government began to loosen its controls on some parts of the economy, in order to reap the economic benefits of freer markets.

As those benefits became clear in higher rates of economic growth and rising standards of living, more government controls were loosened. But, just as market principles were applied to only certain kinds of slavery, so freedom in China has been allowed in economic activities to a far greater extent than in other realms of the country's life, where tight control from the top down remains the norm.

Ironically, the United States is moving in the direction of the kind of economy that China has been forced to move away from. China once had complete government control of medical care, but eventually gave it up as the disaster that it was.

The current leadership in Washington operates as if they can just set arbitrary goals, whether "affordable housing" or "universal health care" or anything else— and not concern themselves with the repercussions— since they have the power to simply force individuals, businesses, doctors or anyone else to knuckle under and follow their dictates.

Friedrich Hayek called this mindset "the road to serfdom." But, even under serfdom and slavery, experience forced those with power to recognize the limits of their power. What this administration— and especially the President— does not have is experience.

Barack Obama had no experience running even the most modest business, and personally paying the consequences of his mistakes, before becoming President of the United States. He can believe that his heady new power is the answer to all things.

Serious or Suicidal?

When you are boating on the Niagara River, there are signs marking the point at which you must go ashore or else you will be sucked over the falls. With Iran moving toward the development of nuclear weapons, we are getting dangerously close to that fatal point of no return on the world stage.

Yet there are few signs of alarm in our public discourse, whether among politicians, the media, or the intelligentsia. There is much more discussion of whether government anti-terrorism agents should be able to look at the records of books borrowed from public libraries.

The Iranian government itself is giving us the clearest evidence of what a nuclear Iran would mean, with its fanatical hate-filled declarations about wanting to wipe Israel off the face of the earth. But send not to know for whom the bell tolls. It tolls for thee.

Just before the 2004 American elections, Osama bin Laden warned that those places that voted for the re-election of President Bush would become targets of terrorist retribution.

We could ignore him then. But neither we, nor our children, nor our children's children will ever be able to ignore him again if he gets nuclear weapons from a nuclear Iran.

We will live at his mercy— of which he has none— if he can wipe out New York or Chicago if we do not knuckle under to his demands, however outrageous those demands might be.

We will truly have passed the point of no return. What will future generations think of us, that we drifted on past the warning signs, preoccupied with library records and with giving foreign terrorists the same legal rights as American citizens?

We could deter the nuclear power of the Soviet Union with our own nuclear power. But you cannot deter suicidal terrorists. You can only kill them or stop them from getting what they need to kill you.

We are killing them in Iraq, though our media seem wholly uninterested in that part of the story, just as they seem uninterested in the fact that the fate of Western civilization may be at stake just across the border in Iran.

Of course they would like us to prevent Iran from going nuclear— if it can be done nicely by diplomacy, with the approval of the U.N., and in ways that do not offend "world opinion."

It is as if we were on the Niagara River and wanted to go ashore before it was too late, but did not want to turn on the motors for fear of disturbing the neighbors with excessive noise.

But at that point, the choice is between being serious or being suicidal.

That is where we are internationally today. Many years ago, there was a book with the title *The Suicide of the West*. It may have been ahead of its time.

The squeamishness, indecision, and wishful thinking of the West are its greatest dangers because the West has the power to destroy any other danger. But it does not have the will.

Partly this is because most of our Western allies have been sheltered from the brutal realities of the international jungle for more than half a century under the American nuclear umbrella. People insulated from dangers for generations can indulge themselves in the illusion that there are no dangers— as much of Western Europe has. This is part of the "world opinion" that makes us hesitant to take any decisive action to prevent a nightmare scenario of nuclear weapons in the hands of hate-filled fanatics.

Do not look for Europe to support any decisive action against Iran. But look for much of their intelligentsia, and much of our own intelligentsia as well, to be alert for any opportunity to wax morally superior if we do act.

They will be able to think of all sorts of nicer alternatives to taking out Iran's nuclear development sites. They will be able to come up with all sorts of abstract arguments and moral equivalence, such as: Other countries have nuclear weapons. Why not Iran?

Debating abstract questions is much easier than confronting concrete and often brutal alternatives. The big question is whether we are serious or suicidal.

Are We France?

One of the painful consequences of studying history is that it makes you realize how long people have been doing the same foolish things with the same disastrous results.

Crowds cheer when Barack Obama declares dramatically that he is going to "bring down the cost of health care," as if price controls were some bright new idea.

There were price controls back in Roman times— and in ancient Babylon before that.

Price controls have had the same bad effects for literally thousands of years. But now they are suddenly the latest "new" formula for salvation.

International "negotiations" are likewise the latest "new" alternative to the use of force. This clever notion has also been tried out before— and with even more disastrous results.

World War II, with tens of millions of people killed, was the result of that clever notion.

After the unprecedented carnage and destruction of the First World War, people could be forgiven for being willing to try anything in hopes of avoiding a repetition.

France was especially hard hit. More Frenchmen were killed in that war than all the Americans ever killed in all our wars put together.

So it is understandable that French foreign minister Aristide Briand was one of the architects of the 1928 international treaty renouncing war— as if renouncing force will do anything other than make you a sitting duck for countries that do not renounce force.

The Kellogg-Briand Pact was just one of the many disarmament treaties and non-aggression pacts that sprang up like mushrooms throughout the 1920s and 1930s.

Nothing is easier than to disarm peaceful people, whether domestically or internationally. But the aggressor nations paid no attention to the agreements they had signed.

For example, one of the consequences of international naval agreements limiting the size of battleships was that Germany and Japan began the Second World War with bigger battleships than either the British or American navies.

We can be charitable toward those who had suffered so much in the First World War that they hoped against hope to avoid going through that again.

But now we know that Utopian, feel-good policies led to even worse horrors in the Second World War. So we have no excuse in our own time— not with nuclear terrorism as a danger looming ahead for ourselves and for generations yet to come.

Even more dangerous than the physical disarmament on which so many pinned their hopes after the First World War was the moral disarmament that took place, especially in France.

History books depicting the heroic French soldiers who had given their lives defending their country against the German invaders were attacked by the

French teachers' union as "bellicose" books that had to be removed from the schools.

Publishers were forced to change their textbooks to reflect the pacifism pervading the teachers' unions, as well as other parts of French society.

Patriotism was out. Internationalism was in, in the name of world peace.

Where previous history books had depicted the epic story of the French soldiers stopping the German invaders at Verdun, despite massive casualties and terrible conditions, the new textbooks depicted Verdun as a scene of horror for *all* soldiers.

"Imagine the suffering of these combatants— French, allies, or enemies," the revisionist history said. French military heroes were reduced to the status of victims— and no better than other victims among the invaders.

A whole generation of Frenchmen raised in the spirit of "moral disarmament" faced a new German invasion in 1940. France, which had held out for four long years in the First World War, collapsed and surrendered after just six weeks of fighting in 1940.

It is something to think about, the next time someone talks about "honoring the troops" when what they are really doing is depicting the troops as victims, and the country they are fighting for as no better than any other.

Notional Security

The latest "screw-up" that let a man with explosives get on a plane on Christmas day is only part of a larger laxness and irresponsibility when it comes to national security. This administration pays lip service to national security and gives out with a lot of rhetorical notions that makes it *notional* security instead of national security.

The Muslim major who was arrested for the murders of American soldiers at Fort Hood had left so many clues to his hatred of this country that all you had to do was count the dots, without even connecting them, to see where he was coming from. But for a fellow officer to alert higher authorities to the danger would have meant risking damage to his own career more so than to that of Major Nidal Hasan.

That is because we have become so obsessed with political correctness that both common sense and self-preservation have to take a back seat. We don't dare "profile" anybody going through security checks because that's not politically correct. Far better to be blown to smithereens than to be politically incorrect.

Probably the country with the strongest security checks for airline passengers— and the strongest reason for such checks— is Israel. Israel profiles. I have been to Israel more than once and it is clear that they profile.

Fortunately, my wife and I obviously don't fit their profile, whatever that may be. Others who have been to Israel are amazed when I tell them that we have gone through Israeli security four times and they have never opened our luggage.

That is all the more surprising, since we take a lot of luggage. We have stopped in Israel while on trips completely around the world, including countries both above and below the equator, so we had to have clothing for hot weather and cold weather, since the seasons are the opposite in the northern and southern hemispheres. Moreover, I carry a lot of photographic equipment in a large, separate piece of luggage.

In short, our luggage could carry enough explosives to blow up any building in the country. But, whatever their security system and whatever their profile, they didn't seem to want to waste any time on us.

The last time we flew into Israel was from Cairo, where the Israeli security officials at the Cairo airport detained the lady in line in front of us for 45 minutes, opened her luggage, spread the contents across the counter, and asked her all sorts of questions. When they had finally finished with her and my wife and I stepped up to the counter, the official in charge waved us on impatiently, saying, "Hurry up, you'll miss the plane."

This was no special treatment for us. They had no idea who we were. We were just not the kind of people they spent time on, for whatever reason.

Recently, an Israeli security official was interviewed on Fox News Channel by Mike Huckabee. The official said that he has testified before Congress and offered to help with suggestions on how the American airport security system could be improved— and he clearly thought it needed a lot of improvement.

Apparently the only response he got from American security officials was a polite letter. "They didn't tell me to go to Hell," he said. "They were polite."

There is no stronger indication of danger than officials who don't want to hear what anybody else has to say, even when those who offer to help have a system that works better than ours.

The fundamental issue goes beyond the Fort Hood massacre or the Christmas bomber. These are just symptoms of a larger set of attitudes and expediencies reflecting the same outlook.

Putting terrorists on trial in American criminal courts, under rules designed for American citizens, tells you all you need to know about whether the Obama administration is serious about security or is still playing the political correctness game.

Terrorists are not covered by the Geneva Convention for the simple reason that they do not abide by the Geneva Convention. They are enemy combatants and you do not turn enemy combatants loose to go back to killing Americans while the war is still on— not if you are being serious, as distinguished from being political or ideological.

A Fatal Trajectory

An increasing number of recent letters and e-mails from readers strike a note, not only of unhappiness with the way things are going in our society, but a note of despair.

Those of us who are pessimists are only a step away from despair ourselves, so we may not be the ones to offer the best antidote to the view that America has seen its best days and is degenerating toward what may well be its worst. Yet what hope remains is no less precious nor any less worthy of being preserved.

First of all, the day-to-day life of most Americans in these times is nowhere near as dire as that of the band of cold, ragged and hungry men who gathered around George Washington in the winter at Valley Forge, to which they had been driven by defeat after defeat.

Only the most reckless gambler would have bet on them to win. Only an optimist would have expected them to survive.

Against the background of those and other desperate times that this country has been through, we cannot whine today because the stocks in our pension plans have gone down or the inflated value that our houses had just a few years ago has now evaporated.

In another sense, however, looming ahead of us— and our children and their children— are dangers that can utterly destroy American society. Worse yet, there are moral corrosions within ourselves that weaken our ability to face the challenges ahead.

One of the many symptoms of this decay from within is that we are preoccupied with the pay of corporate executives while the leading terrorist-sponsoring nation on earth is moving steadily toward creating nuclear bombs.

Does anyone imagine that we will care what anyone's paycheck is when we see an American city in radioactive ruins?

Yet the only serious obstacle to that happening is that the Israelis may disregard the lofty blather coming out of the White House and destroy Iran's nuclear facilities before the Iranian fanatics can destroy Israel.

If by some miracle we manage to avoid the fatal dangers of a nuclear Iran, there will no doubt be others, including a nuclear North Korea.

Although, in some sense, the United States of America is still the militarily strongest nation on earth, that means absolutely nothing if our enemies are willing to die and we are not.

It took only two nuclear bombs to get Japan to surrender— and the Japanese of that era were far tougher than most Americans today. Just one bomb— dropped on New York, Chicago or Los Angeles— might be enough to get us to surrender.

If we are still made of sterner stuff than it looks like, then it might take two or maybe even three or four nuclear bombs, but we will surrender.

It doesn't matter if we retaliate and kill millions of innocent Iranian civilians— at least it will not matter to the fanatics in charge of Iran or the fanatics in charge of the international terrorist organizations that Iran supplies.

Ultimately, it all comes down to who is willing to die and who is not.

How did we get to this point? It was no single thing.

The dumbing down of our education, the undermining of moral values with the fad of "non-judgmental" affectations, the denigration of our nation through poisonous propaganda from the movies to the universities. The list goes on and on.

The trajectory of our course leads to a fate that would fully justify despair. The only saving grace is that even the trajectory of a bullet can be changed by the wind.

We have been saved by miraculous good fortune before in our history. The overwhelming military and naval expedition that Britain sent to New York to annihilate George Washington's army was totally immobilized by a vast impenetrable fog that allowed the Americans to escape. That is how they ended up in Valley Forge.

In the World War II naval battle of Midway, if things had not happened just the way they did, at just the time they did, the American naval force would not only have lost, but could have been wiped out by the far larger Japanese fleet.

Over the years, we have had our share of miraculous deliverances. But that our fate today depends on yet another miracle is what can turn pessimism to despair.

Survival Optional

I t used to be said that self-preservation is the first law of nature. But much of what has been happening in recent times in the United States, and in Western civilization in general, suggests that survival is taking a back seat to the shibboleths of political correctness.

We have already turned loose dozens of captured terrorists, who have resumed their terrorism. Why? Because they have been given "rights" that exist neither in our laws nor under international law.

These are not criminals in our society, entitled to the protection of the Constitution of the United States. They are not prisoners of war entitled to the protection of the Geneva Convention.

There was a time when people who violated the rules of war were not entitled to turn around and claim the protection of those rules. German soldiers who put on U.S. military uniforms, in order to infiltrate American lines during the Battle of the Bulge, were simply lined up against a wall and shot.

Nobody even thought that this was a violation of the Geneva Convention. American authorities filmed the mass executions. Nobody dreamed up fictitious "rights" for these enemy combatants who had violated the rules of war. Nobody thought we had to prove that we were nicer than the Nazis by bending over backward.

Bending over backward is a very bad position from which to try to defend yourself. Nobody in those days confused bending over backward with "the rule of law," as Barack Obama did recently. Bending over backward is the antithesis of the rule of law. It is depriving the people of the protection of their laws, in order to pander to mushy notions among the elite.

Even under the Geneva Convention, enemy soldiers have no right to be turned loose before the war is over. Terrorists— "militants" or "insurgents" for those of you who are squeamish— have declared open-ended war against America. It is open-ended in time and open-ended in methods, including beheadings of innocent civilians.

President Obama can ban the phrase "war on terror" but he cannot ban the terrorists' war on us. That war continues, so there is no reason to turn terrorists loose before it ends. They chose to make it that kind of war. We don't need to risk American lives to prove that we are nicer than they are.

The great Supreme Court justice Oliver Wendell Holmes said that law is not some "brooding omnipresence in the sky." It is a set of explicit rules by which human beings structure their lives and their relationships with one another.

Those who choose to live outside those laws, whether terrorists or pirates, can be— and have been— shot on sight. Squeamishness is neither law nor morality. And moral exhibitionism is beneath contempt, when it sacrifices the safety of those who live within the law for the sake of self-satisfied preening, whether in editorial offices or in the White House.

As if it is not enough to turn cutthroats loose to cut throats again, we are now contemplating legal action against Americans who wrung information about international terrorist operations out of captured terrorists.

Does nobody think ahead to what this will mean— for many years to come— if people trying protect this country from terrorists have to worry about being put behind bars themselves? Do we need to have American intelligence agencies tip-toeing through the tulips when they deal with terrorists?

In his visit to CIA headquarters, President Obama pledged his support to the people working there, and said that there would be no prosecutions of CIA agents for prior actions. Then he welshed on that in a matter of hours by leaving the door open for such prosecutions, which the left has been clamoring for, both inside and outside of Congress.

Repercussions extend far beyond issues of the day. It is bad enough that we have a glib and sophomoric narcissist in the White House. What is worse is that whole nations that rely on the United States for their security see how easily our president welshes on his commitments. So do other nations, including those with murderous intentions toward us, our children and grandchildren.

Words versus Realities

M uch as I hate to be the bearer of bad news, I must report the shocking facts: Medical care is medical care. Nothing more and nothing less.

This may not seem like a breakthrough on the frontiers of knowledge. But it completely contradicts what is being said by many of those who are urging "universal health care" because so many Americans lack health insurance.

Insurance is not medical care. Indeed, health care is not the same as medical care. Countries with universal health care do not have more or better medical care.

The bottom line is medical care. But the rhetoric and the talking points are about insurance. Many people who could afford health insurance do not choose to have it because they know that medical care will be available at the nearest emergency room, whether they have insurance or not.

This is especially true for young people, who do not anticipate long-term medical problems and who can always get a broken leg or an allergy attack taken care of at an emergency room— and spend their money on a more upscale lifestyle.

This may not be a wise decision but it is their decision, and there is no reason why other people should lose the right to make decisions for themselves because some people make questionable decisions.

If you don't think government bureaucrats can make questionable decisions, then you haven't dealt with many government bureaucrats.

It is one thing to deal with bureaucrats when you are at the Department of Motor Vehicles and in good health. It is something else when you have to deal with bureaucrats when you are lying on a gurney and bleeding or are doubled over in pain on a hospital bed.

People who believe in "universal health care" show remarkably little interest— usually none— in finding out what that phrase turns out to mean in practice, in those countries where it already exists, such as Britain, Sweden or Canada.

For one thing, "universal health care" in these countries means months of waiting for surgery that Americans get in a matter of weeks or even days.

In these and other countries, it means having only a fraction as many MRIs and other high-tech medical devices available per person as in the United States.

In Sweden, it means not only having bureaucrats deciding what medicines the government will and will not pay for, but even preventing you from buying the more expensive medicine for yourself with your own money. That would violate the "equality" that is the magic mantra.

Those who think in terms of talking points, instead of trying to understand realities, make much of the fact that some countries with government-controlled medical care have longer life expectancies than that in the United States.

That is where the difference between health care and medical care comes in. Medical care is what doctors can do for you. Health care includes what you do for yourself— such as diet, exercise and lifestyle.

If a doctor arrives on the scene to find you wiped out by a drug overdose or shot through the heart by some of your rougher companions, there may not be much that he can do except sign the death certificate.

Even for things that take longer to do you in— obesity, alcohol, cholesterol, tobacco— doctors can tell you what to do or not do, but whether you follow their advice or not is what determines the outcome.

Americans tend to be more obese, consume more drugs and have more homicides. None of that is going to change with "universal health care" because it isn't health care. It is medical care.

When it comes to things where medical care itself makes the biggest difference— cancer survival rates, for example— Americans do much better than people in most other countries.

No one who compares medical care in this country with medical care in other countries is likely to want to switch. But those who cannot be bothered with the facts may help destroy the best medical care in the world by pursuing a political mirage.

Morally Paralyzed

"Moral paralysis" is a term that has been used to describe the inaction of France, England and other European democracies in the 1930s, as they watched Hitler build up the military forces that he later used to attack them.

It is a term that may be painfully relevant to our own times.

Back in the 1930s, the governments of the democratic countries knew what Hitler was doing— and they knew that they had enough military superiority at that point to stop his military buildup in its tracks. But they did nothing to stop him.

Instead, they turned to what is still the magic mantra today— "negotiations."

No leader of a democratic nation was ever more popular than British Prime Minister Neville Chamberlain— wildly cheered in the House of Commons by opposition parties as well as his own— when he returned from negotiations in Munich in 1938, waving an agreement and declaring that it meant "peace in our time."

We know now how short that time was. Less than a year later, World War II began in Europe and spread across the planet, killing tens of millions of people and reducing many cities to rubble in Europe and Asia.

Looking back after that war, Winston Churchill said, "There was never a war in all history easier to prevent by timely action." The earlier it was done, the less it would have cost.

At one point, Hitler could have been stopped in his tracks "without the firing of a single shot," Churchill said.

That point came in 1936— three years before World War II began— when Hitler sent troops into the Rhineland, in violation of two international treaties.

At that point, France alone was so much more powerful than Germany that the German generals had secret orders to retreat immediately at the first sign of French intervention.

As Hitler himself confided, the Germans would have had to retreat "with our tail between our legs," because they did not yet have enough military force to put up even a token resistance.

Why did the French not act and spare themselves and the world the years of horror that Hitler's aggressions would bring? The French had the means but not the will.

"Moral paralysis" came from many things. The death of a million French soldiers in the First World War and disillusionment with the peace that followed cast a pall over a whole generation.

Pacifism became the vogue among the intelligentsia and spread into educational institutions. As early as 1932, Winston Churchill said: "France, though armed to the teeth, is pacifist to the core."

It was morally paralyzed.

History may be interesting but it is the present and the future that pose the crucial question: Is America today the France of yesterday?

We know that Iran is moving swiftly toward nuclear weapons while the United Nations is moving slowly— or not at all— toward doing anything to stop them.

It is a sign of our irresponsible Utopianism that anyone would even expect the UN to do anything that would make any real difference.

Not only the history of the UN, but the history of the League of Nations before it, demonstrates again and again that going to such places is a way for weak-kneed leaders of democracies to look like they are doing something when in fact they are doing nothing.

The Iranian leaders are not going to stop unless they get stopped. And, like Hitler, they don't think we have the guts to stop them.

Incidentally, Hitler made some of the best anti-war statements of the 1930s. He knew that this was what the Western democracies wanted to hear— and that it would keep them morally paralyzed while he continued building up his military machine to attack them.

Iranian leaders today make only the most token and transparent claims that they are building "peaceful" nuclear facilities— in one of the biggest oil-producing countries in the world, which has no need for nuclear power to generate electricity.

Nuclear weapons in the hands of Iran and its international terrorist allies will be a worse threat than Hitler ever was. But, before that happens, the big question is: Are we France? Are we morally paralyzed, perhaps fatally?

Point of No Return

L ooking back at the history of tragic times often reveals that many— or most— of the people of those times were often preoccupied with things that look trivial, or even pathetic, in view of the catastrophe looming over them. Will later generations looking back at our times see a similar blindness, and even frivolousness, in the face of mortal dangers?

Terrorists and terrorist governments are giving us almost daily evidence of their fanatical hatred and violent sadism, as the clock ticks away toward their gaining possession of nuclear weapons. They not only hold a harmless young woman hostage in Iraq, they parade her in tears on television, just as they have paraded not only the terrorizing, but even the beheading, of others on television.

Moreover, there is a large and gleeful audience in the Arab world for these gross brutalities, just as there was glee and cheering among the Palestinians when the televised destruction of the World Trade Center was broadcast in the Middle East.

Yet what are we preoccupied with or outraged about? Whether the American government should intercept the phone calls of these cutthroats to people in the United States.

That question has been sanitized in the mainstream media by asking whether the government should be engaged in "domestic wiretapping," just as the terrorists themselves have been sanitized into "militants" or "insurgents."

The way the question is posed by many in the media and in politics, you would think our intelligence agencies were listening in on you talking on the phone to your aunt Mabel.

Be serious! There are more than a quarter of a billion people in the United States. Intelligence agencies have neither the manpower, the time, the money, nor the interest to listen in on you and your aunt Mabel.

Lawyers may differ on fine legal points about the Constitutional powers of the commander in chief during wartime versus the oversight powers of the courts. But, a Supreme Court Justice once pointed out that the Constitution of the United States is not a suicide pact.

The Constitution was meant for us to live under, not be paralyzed by, in the face of death.

When some honcho in the international terrorist network is captured in Afghanistan or Iraq, and the phone numbers in his computer are found by his American captors, it is only a matter of time before his capture becomes news broadcast around the world.

In the hour or two before that happens, his contacts within the United States may continue to use the phones they have been using. Listening in on their conversations during that brief window of opportunity can provide valuable information on enemies within our midst who are dedicated to our destruction.

Precious time can be wasted filing legalistic documents to get some judge's permission to tap the domestic terrorists' phones before CBS or CNN broadcasts the news of the captured terrorist leader overseas and the domestic terrorists stop using the phones that they had used before to talk with him.

With Iran advancing step by step toward nuclear weapons, while the Europeans wring their hands and the United Nations engages in leisurely discussion, this squeamishness about tapping terrorists' phone contacts in the United States is grotesque.

Has anyone been paying attention to the audacity of the terrorists? Some in the media seem mildly amused that Palestinian terrorists are threatening Denmark because of editorial cartoons that they found offensive.

Back in the 1930s, some people were amused by Hitler, whose ideas were indeed ridiculous, but by no means funny.

This was not the first threat against a Western country for exercising their freedom in a way that the Islamic fanatics did not like. Osama bin Laden threatened the United States on the eve of our 2004 elections, if we didn't vote the way he wanted.

When he has nuclear weapons, such threats cannot be ignored, when the choice is between knuckling under or seeing American cities blasted off the face of the earth.

That is the point of no return— and we are drifting towards it, chattering away about legalisms and politics.

Something for Nothing?

Suppose someone left you an inheritance of a million dollars— with the proviso that every cent of it had to be spent on tickets for you to go watch professional wrestling matches. If you happened to be a professional wrestling fan, you would be in hog heaven.

But what if you were not? How much would that million dollars be worth to you? Certainly a lot less than a million dollars.

What if there was a clause in the will which said that you could forfeit the million dollars and instead receive a cash amount of $100,000 to spend as you pleased? Many of us would take the hundred grand without strings, even if that was only ten cents on the dollar compared to the million for watching wrestling.

In short, money with strings is worth less than money without strings— sometimes a lot less.

Many of us who receive money from Social Security or other government programs are learning the hard way the difference between money with strings and money without strings. For example, Social Security recipients have to be enrolled in Medicare, whether they want to be or not. "Universal" coverage means compulsory coverage, just with prettier political spin.

Those who are complaining about how hard it is to understand the new Medicare coverage seem not to realize that no government program voted into law by more than 500 members of Congress is going to be simple.

Everybody in Congress has his own pet notions or his own little claim to fame, and a lot of those pet notions and claims to fame have to go into the legislation, in order to get the votes needed to pass the law. The complications and restrictions are the strings attached to Medicare.

People who think that they are getting something for nothing, by having government provide what they would otherwise have to buy in the private market, are not only kidding themselves by ignoring the taxes that government has to take from them in order to give them the appearance of something for nothing. They are also ignoring the strings that are going to be attached to their own money when it comes back to them in government benefits.

That is not even counting the fact that government programs are usually less efficient than similar services provided by private enterprises.

Compare the service you get at the Department of Motor Vehicles with the service you get at Triple-A. No one who belongs to the American Automobile Association is likely to go to the DMV for a service that is also available through Triple-A.

Yet the illusion of something for nothing has kept the welfare state going— and expanding. If there is something for sale in the marketplace for ten dollars and you would not pay more than five dollars for it, some politician can always offer to get it for you free— as a newly discovered "basic right," or at least at a "reasonable" or "affordable" price.

Suppose that the "reasonable" or "affordable" price is three dollars. How do you suppose the government can produce something for three dollars that private industry cannot produce for less than ten dollars? Greater efficiency in government? Give me a break!

The fact that you pay only three dollars at the cash register means nothing. If it costs the government twelve dollars to produce and distribute what you are getting for three dollars, then the government is going to have to get another nine dollars in taxes to cover the difference.

One way or another, you are going to end up paying twelve dollars for something you were unwilling to buy for ten dollars or even six dollars. But so long as you think you are getting something for nothing, the politicians' shell game has worked and the welfare state can continue to expand.

The baby boomers, who are beginning to turn sixty, are unlikely to get back all the money they paid into Social Security, with or without strings. The illusion that Social Security can provide pensions more cheaply than a private annuity or other retirement plan is the grand something-for-nothing political triumph.

The baby boomers are going to pay the price big time.

POLITICAL ISSUES

I f you took all the deception and fraud out of politics, there might not be a lot left. Nor is this peculiar to our country or our time. Back in eighteenth century England, Adam Smith referred to "that insidious and crafty animal, vulgarly called a statesman or politician, whose councils are directed by the momentary fluctuations of affairs." Yet large segments of the public, across the political spectrum, continue to look to political messiahs for "solutions" to our problems.

To understand political issues, you have to understand the incentives facing the politicians who frame those issues and craft "solutions." To expect politicians to put the public interest above their own personal interests is to defy thousands of years of history, in countries around the world.

Exceptional leaders in exceptional times may put the nation's well-being ahead of their own interests. But to bet the survival of a nation on having an unbroken succession of exceptional leaders would be one of the most reckless gambles imaginable. In a democracy, especially, an informed and skeptical citizenry is a crucial bulwark against the short-sighted political expediency which remains as much the norm among crafty politicians today as it was in Adam Smith's time.

One of the trends that can become part of a perfect storm of disasters for American society has been a decades-long dumbing down of education, producing a citizenry poorly equipped to see through political rhetoric, and even more poorly supplied with facts and the ability to analyze opposing arguments.

Thousands of students graduate each year, from even the most prestigious schools and colleges in the country, with no real knowledge of history and no real analytical skills at dissecting opposing views. It was once the proud boast of educators that "We are here to teach you how to think, not what to think." But today, all too many educators see the classroom as a golden opportunity for them to indoctrinate a captive audience.

The specifics of their indoctrination are not the biggest problem. Quite aside from the merits or demerits of the specific indoctrination— whether "global warming" or the new trinity of "race, class and gender"— what the indoctrination process does is get students used to hearing one side of issues and being urged to reach conclusions and act on that grossly inadequate basis. Such an "education" sets them up to become victims of the next skilled demagogue who comes along and who knows what kinds of rhetoric will get them to respond as automatically as Pavlov's dog.

Too often voting is conceived as some sort of expressive outlet for the voters, rather than as a solemn responsibility to pick the best people to lead the country. The emphasis is on getting as high a voter turnout as possible, even if that means pulling into the process people who have only the most meager knowledge or interest in the issues at hand.

Such people cannot preserve freedom, or perhaps even survival, in the face of politicians looking out solely for their advantages of the moment.

Not all political leaders are like that of course. Perhaps the most striking examples to the contrary were the men who created the United States of America and wrote the Constitution. But it is well worth noting that most of these men were *not* career politicians. They had very different careers that they put aside in order to serve in extraordinary and historic times.

We cannot wait for another such remarkable set of leaders and circumstances to come along again, for a whole society can be destroyed from within or without, long before there is such an assemblage of leaders again. When Benjamin Franklin was asked what the Constitutional Convention was producing, he replied, "A republic, madam— if you can keep it." Those who wrote the Constitution of the United States understood that a self-governing society was an experiment, and one that was not guaranteed against failure. Generations later, Abraham Lincoln raised the question whether "government of the people, by the people and for the people shall not perish from the earth." Today, perhaps more so than ever, it is the people who ultimately will provide the answer to that question— and that answer is by no means guaranteed.

The Art of the Impossible

Whoever called politics "the art of the possible" must have had a strange idea of what is possible or a strange idea of politics, where the impossible is one of the biggest vote-getters.

People can get the possible on their own. Politicians have to be able to offer the voters something that they cannot get on their own. The impossible fills that bill perfectly.

As a noted economist has pointed out, nothing "could prevent the California electorate from simultaneously demanding low electricity prices and no new generating plants while using ever increasing amounts of electricity."

You want the impossible? You got it. Politicians don't get elected by saying "No" to voters.

Of course Californians also got electricity blackouts and, in order to deal with the blackouts, a multi-billion dollar surplus in the state's treasury was turned into a multi-billion dollar deficit, followed by cutbacks in various other government programs, followed by calls for higher taxes.

You want the government to create more jobs for people when there is widespread unemployment? It's been done. During the Great Depression of the 1930s, the government employed more young men in the Civilian Conservation Corps than there were in the Army. The money to pay for all this had to come from somewhere— and that meant that there was less money left to employ other people in the private sector. While jobs created by the government may not have reduced total unemployment, these jobs increased votes for the administration, which is the real bottom line in politics.

Are you for "open space" laws forbidding building and also for "affordable housing"? Don't be discouraged by the fact that severe building restrictions have sent housing prices sky-rocketing in community after community.

It may be impossible to have "open space" laws and "affordable housing" at the same time, but what are politicians there for, except to figure out ways to give us the impossible?

Palo Alto, California, where housing prices nearly quadrupled in one decade after severe building restrictions were imposed, also pioneered in laws mandating that each builder agree to sell a certain percentage of any new housing "below market."

In other words, they combined "open space" laws with "affordable housing." Who says the impossible cannot be achieved?

Of course this system can work only where just a fraction of the new housing is sold "below market." Moreover, the market price of housing was raised so far above what it was by building restrictions that even "below market" prices for condominiums in Palo Alto can run to $300,000 or $400,000.

This is hardly "affordable housing" for people on modest incomes. Only 7 percent of Palo Alto's police, for example, live in Palo Alto— probably older cops who bought their homes long ago.

But none of that matters politically. What matters is that people in Palo Alto can feel good about themselves, by being for both "open space" and "affordable housing." Happy voters are what get politicians re-elected.

The big political crusade today is for "affordable" medical care through the government. No one believes that government is just going to be more efficient, and thereby have lower costs that will be reflected in lower prices for medications and medical treatment.

It might seem as if adding the costs of government bureaucracies to the costs of medications and medical treatment would make it impossible for the total costs to go down. But again, the impossible is no problem in politics.

Many countries around the world already have government-run medical care. People who get sick in these countries usually wait much longer to get treatment, including months on waiting lists for surgery, often paying in pain or debilitation, rather than in money.

High-tech medical devices like MRIs are also far less common in these countries than in the United States. With medical care as with anything else, you can always get poorer quality at a lower price, though that is no bargain, especially when you are sick.

What you may have in mind are lower prices with no reduction in quality. While that may be impossible, don't expect that fact to stop politicians from offering it, even if they can't deliver.

Solving Whose Problem?

No one will really understand politics until they understand that politicians are not trying to solve our problems. They are trying to solve their own problems— of which getting elected and re-elected are number one and number two. Whatever is number three is far behind.

Many of the things the government does that may seem stupid are not stupid at all, from the standpoint of the elected officials or bureaucrats who do these things.

The current economic downturn that has cost millions of people their jobs began with successive administrations of both parties pushing banks and other lenders to make mortgage loans to people whose incomes, credit history and inability or unwillingness to make a substantial down payment on a house made them bad risks.

Was that stupid? Not at all. The money that was being put at risk was not the politicians' money, and in most cases was not even the government's money. Moreover, the jobs that are being lost by the millions are not the politicians' jobs— and jobs in the government's bureaucracies are increasing.

No one pushed these reckless mortgage lending policies more than Congressman Barney Frank, who brushed aside warnings about risk, and said in 2003 that he wanted to "roll the dice" even more in the housing markets. But it would be very rash to bet against Congressman Frank's getting re-elected in 2010.

After the cascade of economic disasters that began in the housing markets in 2006 and spread into the financial markets in Wall Street and even overseas, people in the private sector pulled back. Banks stopped making so many risky loans. Home buyers began buying homes they could afford, instead of going out on a limb with "creative"— and risky— financing schemes to buy homes that were beyond their means.

But politicians went directly in the opposite direction. In the name of "rescuing" the housing market, Congress passed laws enabling the Federal Housing Administration to insure more and bigger risky loans— loans where there is less than a 4 percent down payment.

A recent news story told of three young men who chipped in a total of $33,000 to buy a home in San Francisco that cost nearly a million dollars. Why would a bank lend that kind of money to them on such a small down payment? Because the loan was insured by the Federal Housing Administration.

The bank wasn't taking any risk. If the three guys defaulted, the bank could always collect the money from the Federal Housing Administration. The only risk was to the taxpayers.

Does the Federal Housing Administration have unlimited money to bail out bad loans? Actually there have been so many defaults that the FHA's own reserves have dropped below where they are supposed to be. But not to worry. There will always be taxpayers, not to mention future generations, to pay off the national debt.

Very few people are likely to connect the dots back to those members of Congress who voted for bigger mortgage guarantees and bailouts by the FHA. So the Congressmen's and the bureaucrats' jobs are safe, even if millions of other people's jobs are not.

Congressman Barney Frank is not about to cut back on risky mortgage loan guarantees by the FHA. He recently announced that he plans to introduce legislation to raise the limit on FHA loan guarantees even more.

Congressman Frank will make himself popular with people who get those loans and with banks that make these high-risk loans where they can pocket the profits and pass the risk on to the FHA.

So long as the taxpayers don't understand that all this political generosity and compassion are at their expense, Barney Frank is an odds-on favorite to get re-elected. The man is not stupid.

What is stupid is believing that politicians are trying to solve our problems, instead of theirs.

As for the FHA running low on money, that is not about to stop the gravy train, certainly not with an election coming up in 2010.

The Federal Deposit Insurance Corporation is also running low on money. But that is not going to stop them from insuring bank accounts up to a quarter of a million dollars. It would be stupid for them to stop with an election coming up in 2010.

It's Priceless

Wouldn't it be wonderful to live in a world where there were no prices?

If you happened to want a Rolex or a Rolls-Royce, you could just go get one— or two if you wanted— and not have to worry about ugly little things like price tags.

There is such a world. It is the world of political rhetoric. No wonder so many people are attracted to that world. It would be a great place to live.

After Arthur Goldberg had served on the Supreme Court, he lamented that more of society's problems could not be dealt with as that court dealt with them— by reaching a decision and then declaring, "It is so ordered."

Politics offers something similar. Theoretically, political decisions are limited by budgets. But for many experienced politicians, that limit is mostly theoretical.

Government budgets, after all, are only projections of what is supposed to happen, not a hard and fast record of what has in fact happened. And seldom will the public or the media do anything so mean-spirited as go back and compare what the budget said would happen with what actually happened.

Moreover, politicians can put certain large expenditures "off budget" for any number of noble-sounding reasons. And if you have long experience in using political rhetoric, nothing is easier than coming up with noble-sounding reasons.

If you could put it "off budget," wouldn't you buy a second home at the beach or maybe a yacht to go out on the water? Why not live a little— or a lot?

Politicians have more ways of escaping from prices than Houdini had ways of escaping from locks. When savvy pols want to hand out goodies, but don't want to take responsibility for raising taxes to pay for them, they can tax people who can't vote— namely the next generation— by getting the money by selling government bonds that future taxpayers will have to redeem.

Even such deficit spending leaves a record, however— a national debt that is the ghost of Christmas past. But politicians can even get around that.

The most politically painless way to hand out goodies, without taking responsibility for their costs, is to pass a law saying that somebody else must provide those goodies at their expense, while the politicians take credit for generosity and compassion.

Employers are ideal targets for such mandates, since there are always more employees than employers, and that is what counts on election day. Whether it is health insurance, time off with pay or whatever, these mandates on employers can be washed down with a little rhetoric about business' "social responsibilities."

Where those "social responsibilities" come from is not a problem. It sounds good, and that is good enough for politics.

Some people may go away mad if they are ignored. Costs are not like that. You can ignore them all you want and they still won't go away.

While you are enjoying all the goodies that politicians are sending your way, you may notice that your taxes are going up or that the money you earn or the money you have saved won't buy as much as it used to.

Costs that are passed on to businesses can get passed on again to their customers in higher prices. Money that the government prints to spend itself reduces the value of the money in your wallet or in your bank account.

If you are someone looking for a job— maybe a young person entering the labor force or a woman coming back into the labor force after spending a few years taking care of a small child— you may find that there aren't as many jobs available as there used to be before employers had to pay for "social responsibilities," in addition to paying for the value of an employee's work.

Desperate times can call for desperate measures, so maybe you will try to find out from some economist what is going on. You may not get any much better explanation than "There is no free lunch"— which is one of many reasons why economists are not popular.

But there really is no free lunch, except in the world of political rhetoric, a world that so many want to be in, where they can play Santa Claus without even paying the cost of buying a costume.

Inept Republicans

S ome people say that there is no real difference between Republicans and Democrats. Whether that is said because of being too lazy to examine the differences or because it makes some people feel exalted to say, in effect, "a plague on both your houses," it is a dangerous self-indulgence.

When Republicans were in power, they acted too much like Democrats, with big spending and earmarks, lending weight to the notion that there is no real difference.

Among the differences between the parties is that Democrats are more articulate.

Admittedly, the Democrats have an easier case to make. It takes no great amount of thought, nor much in the way of persuasive powers, to sell the idea of government handing out benefits hither and yon. It is only when you stop and think about the consequences, for this generation and generations to come, that some grim questions arise.

But if Republicans don't raise those awkward questions, and don't take the trouble to explain what is wrong with government playing Santa Claus, then the Democrats can soar on a cloud of euphoria.

Sometimes it doesn't matter that you have a better product, if your competitors have better salesmen.

Republicans lag not only in the articulation department, they also lag in seeing the long-run importance of the federal bureaucracy. When the Democrats load the federal bureaucracy with liberals, those liberals stay on during Republican administrations and in many cases can shape the perceptions that reach the media and the public, by the way they present data, hire consultants and make grants.

The Bureau of the Census is a classic example. The tendentious way that data and pie charts are presented provides a steady stream of material for a political and media drumbeat about "disparities" that call for government intervention.

Data on income differences, for example, are presented in a way that suggests that the different income brackets represent enduring classes of people over time, when in fact other studies show that the vast majority of people in the lowest income brackets as of a given time rise out of those brackets over time. More people from the bottom fifth end up in the top fifth than remain at the bottom.

Household income data are presented in ways which suggest that there is very little real improvement in the American people's standard of living over time, and innumerable editorials and television commentaries have elaborated that theme. But per capita income data show far more improvement over time. The difference is that households have been getting smaller but one person always means one person.

Just by deciding what kind of data to present in what way, the Census Bureau has become, in effect, an adjunct of the liberal establishment, even when conservative Republicans are in control of the federal government. This is not necessarily deliberate political sabotage, just liberals being liberals.

Robert Rector of the Heritage Foundation has for years repeatedly exposed the fallacies of the inferences drawn from Census data.

Yet when Republicans controlled the federal government— as they did for 12 consecutive years, beginning in 1981— did they try to appoint someone like Robert Rector to a position where they could put an end to tendentious statistics that promote misconceptions with political implications? Not at all.

Too many Republicans don't even know their own party's history. One painful consequence is that too many Republicans act as if they have to apologize for their party's civil rights record— which is in fact better than that of the Democrats.

A higher percentage of Republicans than Democrats voted for the Civil Rights Act of 1964 and the Voting Rights Act of 1965. It was Republicans whose "Philadelphia Plan" in the 1970s sought to break the construction unions' racial barriers that kept blacks out of skilled trades.

Just as boxers have to do training in the gym and roadwork before they are ready for a boxing match, Republicans need to do a lot of homework before they are ready for their next match against the Democrats.

The Brainy Bunch

M any people, including some conservatives, have been very impressed with how brainy the president and his advisers are. But that is not quite as reassuring as it might seem.

It was, after all, Franklin D. Roosevelt's brilliant "brains trust" advisers whose policies are now increasingly recognized as having prolonged the Great Depression of the 1930s, while claiming credit for ending it. The Great Depression ended only when the Second World War put an end to many New Deal policies.

FDR himself said that "Dr. New Deal" had been replaced by "Dr. Win-the-War." But those today who are for big spending like to credit wartime big spending for bringing the Great Depression to an end. They never ask the question as to why previous depressions had always ended on their own, much faster than the one under FDR, and without government intervention or massive government spending.

Brainy folks were also present in Lyndon Johnson's administration, especially in the Pentagon, where Secretary of Defense Robert McNamara's brilliant "whiz kids" tried to micro-manage the Vietnam war, with disastrous results.

There is usually only a limited amount of damage that can be done by dull or stupid people. For creating a truly monumental disaster, you need people with high IQs.

Such people have been told all their lives how brilliant they are, until finally they feel forced to admit it, with all due modesty. But they not only tend to over-estimate their own brilliance, more fundamentally they tend to over-estimate how important brilliance itself is when dealing with real world problems.

Many crucial things in life are learned from experience, rather than from clever thoughts or clever words. Indeed, a gift for the clever phrasing so much admired by the media can be a fatal talent, especially for someone chosen to lead a government.

Make no mistake about it, Adolf Hitler was brilliant. His underlying beliefs may have been half-baked and his hatreds overwhelming, but he was a genius when it came to carrying out his plans politically, based on those beliefs and hatreds.

Starting from a position of Germany's military weakness in the early 1930s, Hitler not only built up Germany's war-making potential, he did so in ways that minimized the danger that his potential victims would match his military build-up with their own. He said whatever soothing words they wanted to hear that would spare them the cost of military deterrence and the pain of contemplating another war.

He played some of the most highly educated people of his time for fools— not only foreign political leaders but also members of the intelligentsia. The editor of *The Times* of London filtered out reports that his own foreign correspondents in Germany sent him about the evils and dangers of the Nazis. In the United States,

W.E.B. Du Bois— with a Ph.D. from Harvard— said that dictatorship in Germany was "absolutely necessary to get the state in order."

In an age when facts seem to carry less weight than the visions of brilliant and charismatic leaders, it is more important than ever to look at the actual track records of those brilliant and charismatic leaders. After all, Hitler led Germany into military catastrophe and left much of the country in ruins.

Even in a country which suffered none of the wartime destruction that others suffered in the 20th century, Argentina began that century as one of the 10 richest nations in the world— ahead of France and Germany— and ended it as such an economic disaster that no one would even compare it to France or Germany.

Politically brilliant and charismatic leaders, promoting reckless government spending— of whom Juan Peron was the most prominent, but by no means alone— managed to create an economic disaster in a country with an abundance of natural resources and a country that was spared the stresses that wars inflicted on other nations in the 20th century.

Someone recently pointed out how much Barack Obama's style and strategies resemble those of Latin American charismatic despots— the takeover of industries by demagogues who never ran a business, the rousing rhetoric of resentment addressed to the masses and the personal cult of the leader promoted by the media. But do we want to become the world's largest banana republic?

Mascot Politics

Years ago, when Jack Greenberg left the NAACP Legal Defense Fund to become a professor at Columbia University, he announced that he was going to make it a point to hire a black secretary at Columbia.

This would of course make whomever he hired be seen as a token black, rather than as someone selected on the basis of competence.

This reminded me of the first time I went to Milton Friedman's office, when I was a graduate student at the University of Chicago back in 1960, and I noticed that he had a black secretary. This was four years before the Civil Rights Act of 1964, and there was no such thing as affirmative action.

Milton Friedman had the same black secretary decades later when he moved to the Hoover Institution— and she was respected as one of the best secretaries around.

When I mentioned to someone at the Hoover Institution that I was having a hard time finding a secretary who could handle a tough job in my absence, I was told that I needed someone like Milton Friedman's secretary— and that there were not many like her.

At no time in all these years did I hear Milton Friedman mention, either publicly or privately, that he had a black secretary.

William F. Buckley's wife once mentioned in passing, at dinner in her home, that she had been involved for years in working with a school in Harlem. But I never heard her or Bill Buckley ever say that publicly.

Nor do conservatives who were in the civil rights marches in the South, back when that was dangerous, make that a big deal.

For people on the left, however, blacks are trophies or mascots, and must therefore be put on display. Nowhere is that more true than in politics.

The problem with being a mascot is that you are a symbol of someone else's significance or virtue. The actual well-being of a mascot is not the point. Liberals all across the country have not hesitated to destroy black neighborhoods in the name of "urban renewal," often replacing working-class neighborhoods with upscale homes and pricey businesses— neither of which the former residents can afford.

In academia, lower admissions standards for black students are about having them as a visible presence, even if mismatching them with the particular college or university produces high dropout rates.

The black students who don't make it are replaced by others, and when many of them don't make it either, there are still more others.

The point is to have black faces on campus, as mascots symbolizing what great people there are running the college or university.

Many, if not most, of the black students who do not make it at big-name, high-pressure institutions are perfectly qualified to succeed at the normal range of colleges and universities.

Most white students would also punch out if admitted to schools for which they don't have the same qualifications as the other students. But nobody needs white mascots.

Various empirical studies have indicated that blacks succeed best at institutions where there is little or no difference between their qualifications and the qualifications of the other students around them.

This is not rocket science but it is amazing how much effort and cleverness have gone into denying the obvious.

A study by Professor Richard Sander of the UCLA law school suggests that there may be fewer black lawyers as a result of "affirmative action" admissions to law schools that are a mismatch for the individuals admitted.

Leaping to the defense of black criminals is another common practice among liberals who need black mascots. Most of the crimes committed by black criminals are committed against other blacks. But, again, the actual well-being of mascots is not the point.

Politicians who use blacks as mascots do not hesitate to throw blacks to the wolves for the benefit of the teachers' unions, the green zealots whose restrictions make housing unaffordable, or people who keep low-price stores like Wal-Mart out of their cities.

Using human beings as mascots is not idealism. It is self-aggrandizement that is ugly in both its concept and its consequences.

Utopia versus Freedom

" Eternal vigilance is the price of freedom." We have heard that many times. What is also the price of freedom is the toleration of imperfections. If everything that is wrong with the world becomes a reason to turn more power over to some political savior, then freedom is going to erode away, while we are mindlessly repeating the catchwords of the hour, whether "change," "universal health care" or "social justice."

If we can be so easily stampeded by rhetoric that neither the public nor the Congress can be bothered to read, much less analyze, bills making massive changes in medical care, then do not be surprised when life and death decisions about you or your family are taken out of your hands— and out of the hands of your doctor— and transferred to bureaucrats in Washington.

Let's go back to square one. The universe was not made to our specifications. Nor were human beings. So there is nothing surprising in the fact that we are dissatisfied with many things at many times. The big question is whether we are prepared to follow any politician who claims to be able to "solve" our "problem."

If we are, then there will be a never ending series of "solutions," each causing new problems calling for still more "solutions." That way lies a never-ending quest, costing ever increasing amounts of the taxpayers' money and— more important— ever greater losses of your freedom to live your own life as you see fit, rather than as presumptuous elites dictate.

Ultimately, our choice is to give up Utopian quests or give up our freedom. This has been recognized for centuries by some, but many others have not yet faced that reality, even today. If you think government should "do something" about anything that ticks you off, or anything you want and don't have, then you have made your choice between Utopia and freedom.

Back in the 18th century, Edmund Burke said, "It is no inconsiderable part of wisdom, to know much of an evil ought to be tolerated" and "I must bear with infirmities until they fester into crimes."

But today's crusading zealots are not about to tolerate evils or infirmities. If insurance companies are not behaving the way some people think they should, then their answer is to set up a government bureaucracy to either control insurance companies or replace them.

If doctors, hospitals or pharmaceutical companies charge more than some people feel like paying, then the answer is price control. The actual track record of politicians, government bureaucracies, or price control is of no interest to those who think this way.

Politicians are already one of the main reasons why medical insurance is so expensive. Insurance is designed to cover risks but politicians are in the business of distributing largesse. Nothing is easier for politicians than to mandate things that insurance companies must cover, without the slightest regard for how such additional coverage will raise the cost of insurance.

If insurance covered only those things that most people are most concerned about— such as the high cost of a major medical expense— the price would be much lower than it is today, with politicians piling on mandate after mandate.

Since insurance covers risks, there is no reason for it to cover annual checkups, because it is known in advance that annual checkups occur once a year. Automobile insurance does not cover oil changes, much less the purchase of gasoline, since these are regular recurrences, not risks.

But politicians in the business of distributing largesse— especially with somebody else's money— cannot resist the temptation to pass laws adding things to insurance coverage. Many of those who are pushing for more government involvement in medical care are already talking about extending insurance coverage to "mental health"— which is to say, giving shrinks and hypochondriacs a blank check drawn on the federal treasury.

There are still some voices of sanity today, echoing what Edmund Burke said long ago. "The study of human institutions is always a search for the most tolerable imperfections," according to Prof. Richard Epstein of the University of Chicago. If you cannot tolerate imperfections, be prepared to kiss your freedom goodbye.

Magic Words in Politics

China is the largest foreign holder of U.S. government bonds. But, instead of buying more of those bonds as our skyrocketing national debt leads to more bonds being issued, China has been selling some of its U.S. government bonds this year.

The Chinese are no fools. They know that all this unbridled spending— even when it is called "investment"— means that inflation is coming. That in turn means that the dollars with which U.S. government bonds will be paid off will be worth a lot less than the dollars with which the bonds were bought.

Governments around the world have played this game for centuries, robbing those who trusted them enough to buy their bonds. Like Bernard Madoff, they call it "investment."

Inflation also means that all the talk about how higher taxes will be confined to "the rich" is nonsense. Inflation is a hidden tax that takes away the value of money held by everyone at every income level.

Abraham Lincoln once asked an audience how many legs a dog has if you count the tail as a leg. When they answered "five," Lincoln told them that the answer was four. The fact that you called the tail a leg did not make it a leg.

It is too bad that Lincoln is not still around today. He might emancipate us all from our enslavement to words.

When you call something a "stimulus" package, that does not mean that it actually stimulates. The way individuals, banks and businesses in general are hanging on to their money suggests that "sedative" package might be more accurate.

This is not a new phenomenon, peculiar to this administration. President Bush's "stimulus" package did not stimulate either. The same was true back in the days of Franklin D. Roosevelt's "pump-priming" by spending government money to get private money flowing.

The circulation of money slowed down back then the way it has slowed down today.

Some of our biggest political fallacies come from accepting words as evidence of realities. "Rent control" laws do not control rent and "gun control" laws do not control guns.

The big cities with the tightest rent control laws in the nation are New York and San Francisco. The nation's highest rents are in New York and the second-highest are in San Francisco.

There is a very straightforward explanation for that. Strong rent control laws can bring residential building to a screeching halt. Once politicians have milked the political advantages of passing rent control laws, they have to avoid a backlash if all building of apartments stops.

That leads to an escape hatch in the rent control law. Luxury apartments with rents above a certain level are exempted. That leads to the shifting of resources away from building affordable housing to building luxury housing.

It is even more painfully obvious that "gun control" laws do not control guns. The District of Columbia's very strong laws against gun ownership have done nothing to stop the high murder rate in Washington.

New York had very strong gun control laws decades before London did. But the murder rate in New York has been some multiple of that in London for more than two centuries, regardless of which city had the stronger gun control laws at a given time.

Back in 1954, when there were no restrictions on owning shotguns in England and there were far more owners of pistols then than there were decades later, there were only 12 cases of armed robbery in London.

By the 1990s, after stringent gun controls laws were imposed, there were well over a thousand armed robberies a year in London. In the late 1990s, after an almost total ban on handguns in England, gun crimes went up another ten percent.

The reason— too obvious to be accepted by the intelligentsia— is that law-abiding people became more defenseless against criminals who ignored the law and kept their guns.

The same thing applies internationally. We might keep that in mind as the Obama administration pursues the will o' the wisp of banning nuclear weapons. If that Utopian dream ever came true, those nations naive enough to get rid of their nuclear weapons would be at the mercy of those rogue states who kept theirs.

A War of Words

It has long been recognized that those on the political left are more articulate than their opponents. The words they choose for the things they are for or against make it easy to decide whether to be for or against those things.

Are you for or against "social justice"? A no-brainer. Who is going to be for injustice?

What about "a living wage"? Who wants people not to have enough money to live on?

Then there is "affordable housing" and "affordable health care." Who would want people to be unable to afford to put a roof over their heads or unable to go to a doctor when they are sick?

In real life, the devil is in the details. But the whole point of political rhetoric is to make it unnecessary for you to have to go into the specifics before taking sides.

You don't need to know any economics to be in favor of "a living wage" or "affordable housing." In fact, the less economics you know, the more you can believe in such things.

Conservatives, on the other hand, have a gift for phrasing things in terms that are unlikely to arouse most people's interest, much less their support.

Do words like "property rights," "the market" or "judicial restraint" make your emotions surge and your heart beat faster?

There are serious reasons to be greatly concerned about all these things. But you have to have a lot more facts and more understanding of history, economics, and law before you see why.

An issue can be enormously important and well within most people's understanding. Yet the way words are used can determine whether people are aroused or bored.

One of those issues is what legal scholars call "takings." There is a masterful book with that title by Professor Richard Epstein of the University of Chicago Law School.

But if you are in a bookstore and see a book with the title *Takings* on its cover, are you more likely to stop in your tracks and eagerly snatch it off the shelf or to yawn and keep walking?

Takings are not a complex idea. But it needs explaining.

Let's suppose you live in a $400,000 house.

If, on a Wednesday afternoon, the government announces that it is planning to "redevelop" the area where your home is located— that is, demolish the area so that something else can be built there— by Thursday morning, your $400,000 house could become a $200,000 house.

The market reacts very quickly in anticipation of future events.

Several years later, when the government actually gets around to demolishing the area, they may offer you $200,000 for your property— or perhaps $150,000, if they use an appraiser who knows that he is more likely to get more business from the government if his estimates are on the low side rather than the high side.

In either case, you are out at least a couple of hundred grand. Has the government "taken" that much from you, without paying you the full compensation for your property, as required by the Constitution of the United States?

Such theoretical questions were made vividly real, and people were lividly outraged, when the Supreme Court in 2005 declared that governments at all levels had the power to seize private property, not only for such government activities as building reservoirs or highways, but also for turning the property over to private developers to build shopping malls, casinos, or whatever.

The Constitution says that government can take private property for "public use" if it compensates the owner. The Supreme Court changed that to mean that the government could take private property just to turn it over to others, so long as they called it a "public purpose" like "redevelopment."

Politicians are experts at rhetoric, especially if that is all that is needed to justify seizing your home and turning it over to someone else who will build something that pays more taxes.

All hell broke out, once people now understood that the issue called "takings" was about politicians being able to seize their property, virtually at will, for someone else's benefit. But it was a liberal court decision, not the words of conservatives, which created that understanding.

Republicans in the Wilderness

A Gallup poll last week showed that far more Americans describe themselves as "conservatives" than as "liberals." Yet Republicans have been clobbered by the Democrats in both the 2006 elections and the 2008 elections.

In a country with more conservatives than liberals, it is puzzling— in fact, amazing— that we have the furthest left President of the United States in history, as well as the furthest left Speaker of the House of Representatives.

Republicans, especially, need to think about what this means. If you lose when the other guy has all the high cards, there is not much you can do about it. But, when you have the high cards and still keep taking a beating, then you need to re-think how you are playing the game.

The current intramural fighting among Republicans does not necessarily mean any fundamental re-thinking of their policies or tactics. These tussles among different segments of the Republican Party may be nothing more than a long-standing jockeying for position between the liberal and conservative wings of that party.

The stakes in all this are far higher than which element becomes dominant in which party or which party wins more elections. Both the domestic and the foreign policy direction of the current administration in

Washington are leading this country into dangerous waters, from which we may or may not be able to return.

A tripling of the federal deficit in just one year and accepting a nuclear-armed sponsor of international terrorism like Iran are not things from which any country is guaranteed to recover.

Just two nuclear bombs were enough to get Japan to surrender in World War II. It is hard to believe that it would take much more than that for the United States of America to surrender— especially with people in control of both the White House and the Congress who were for turning tail and running in Iraq just a couple of years ago.

Perhaps people who are busy gushing over the Obama cult today might do well to stop and think about what it would mean for their grand-daughters to live under Sharia law.

The glib pieties in Barack Obama's televised sermonettes will not stop Iran from becoming a nuclear terrorist nation. Time is running out fast and we will be lucky if it doesn't happen in the first term of this president. If he gets elected to a second term— which is quite possible, despite whatever economic disasters he leads us into— our fate as a nation may be sealed.

Unfortunately, the only political party with any chance of displacing the current leadership in Washington is the Republican Party. That is why their internal squabbles are important for the rest of us who are not Republicans.

The "smart money" says that the way for the Republicans to win elections is to appeal to a wider range of voters, including minorities, by abandoning the Ronald Reagan kinds of positions and supporting more of the kinds of positions that Democrats use to get elected. This sounds good on the surface, which is as far as many people go, when it comes to politics.

A corollary to this is that Republicans have to come up with alternatives to the Democrats' many "solutions," rather than simply be nay-sayers.

However plausible all this may seem, it goes directly counter to what has actually happened in politics in this generation. For example, Democrats studiously avoided presenting alternatives to what the Republican-controlled Congress and the Bush administration were doing, and just lambasted them at every turn. That is how the Democrats replaced Republicans at both ends of Pennsylvania Avenue.

Ronald Reagan won two elections in a landslide by being Ronald Reagan and— most important of all— explaining to a broad electorate how what he advocated would be best for them and for the country. Newt Gingrich likewise led a Republican takeover of the House of Representatives by explaining how the Republican agenda would benefit a wide range of people.

Neither of them won by pretending to be Democrats. It is the mushy "moderates"— the "kinder and gentler" Bush 41, Bob Dole and John McCain— who lost disastrously, even in two cases to Democrats who were initially very little known, but who knew how to talk.

Burke and Obama

The other day I sought a respite from current events by re-reading some of the writings of 18th century British statesman Edmund Burke. But it was not nearly as big an escape as I had thought it would be.

When Burke wrote of his apprehension about "new power in new persons," I could not help think of the new powers that have been created by which a new President of the United States— a man with zero experience in business— can fire the head of General Motors and tell banks how to run their businesses.

Not only is Barack Obama new to the presidency, he is new to running any organization. One of Burke's fears was that "we may place our confidence in the virtue of those who have never been tried."

Neither eloquence nor zeal was a substitute for experience, according to Burke. He said, "eloquence may exist without a proportionate degree of wisdom." As for zeal, Burke said: "It is no excuse for presumptuous ignorance that it is directed by insolent passion."

The Obama administration's going back and forth on the question whether American intelligence agents who forced information out of captured terrorist leaders will be subjected to legal jeopardy, even though they were told at the time that what they were doing was not only legal but a service to the nation, came to mind when reading Burke's warning about the dangers of continuing to change the rules and values by which people lived.

Burke asked how we could expect a sense of honor to exist when "no man could know what would be the test of honour in a nation, continually varying the standard of its coin?"

The current drive to take from "the rich" for the benefit of others came to mind when reading Burke's warning against creating a situation where "any one description of citizens should be brought to regard any of the others as their proper prey."

He also warned that "those who attempt to level, never equalise." What they end up doing is concentrating power in their own hands— and Burke saw such new powers as dangerous, even if they were used only sparingly at first.

He said, "the true danger is, when liberty is nibbled away, for expedients and by parts." He also said: "It is by lying dormant a long time, or being at first very rarely exercised, that arbitrary power steals upon a people."

People who don't like "the rich" or "big business" or the banks may be happy that President Obama is sticking it to them. But such arbitrary powers can be turned on anybody. As John Donne said: "Send not to know for whom the bell tolls. It tolls for thee."

The Constitution of the United States set out to limit the powers of the federal government but judges have greatly eroded those limitations over the years and the dispensing of bailout money has allowed the Obama administration to exercise powers that the Constitution never gave them.

Edmund Burke understood that, no matter what form of government you had, in the end the character of those who wielded the powers of government was crucial. He said: "Constitute government how you please, infinitely the greater part of it must depend upon the exercise of the powers which are left at large to the prudence and uprightness of ministers of state."

He also said, "of all things, we ought to be the most concerned who and what sort of men they are that hold the trust of everything that is dear to us." He feared particularly the kind of man "whose whole importance has begun with his office, and is sure to end with it"— the kind of man "who before he comes into power has no friends, or who coming into power is obliged to desert his friends." Jeremiah Wright, Bill Ayers and others came to mind.

The biggest challenge to America— and to the world— today is the danger of Iran with nuclear weapons. President Obama is acting as if this is something he can finesse with talks or deals. Worse yet, he may think it is something we can live with.

Burke had something to say about things like that as well: "There is no safety for honest men, but by believing all possible evil of evil men, and by acting with promptitude, decision, and steadiness on that belief." Acting— not talking.

Oily Politics

The Supreme Court's recent [2006] unanimous decision shot down a claim that oil companies were colluding in setting prices. That claim was upheld by the far-left 9th Circuit Court of Appeals but neither liberals nor conservatives on the Supreme Court were buying it.

This unanimous vote should also tell us something about those politicians who are forever blaming rising gasoline prices on oil company collusion and "greed." There is no point exposing a lie unless we learn to be skeptical the next time the liars come out with the same story.

After hurricane Katrina destroyed a lot of oil processing capacity around the Gulf of Mexico, there was— surprise!— less oil being processed. With less oil being supplied— surprise again!— gasoline prices rose.

However much economists rely on supply and demand to explain price movements, politicians need villains, so that the pols can play hero. Big Oil is a favorite villain and has been for decades.

There is nothing like the political melodrama of summoning oil company executives to televised hearings before some Congressional committee, where politicians can wax indignant at Big Oil's profits.

It so happens that Big Government takes more money in taxes out of a gallon of gas than Big Oil takes out in profits. But apparently somehow taxes don't raise prices. They certainly don't raise indignation from the politicians who voted for those taxes.

After the oil processing facilities were repaired and put back in operation— yet another surprise!— prices came back down. Supply and demand have been doing this for centuries but apparently the word has not yet reached some politicians.

There is another aspect to supply and demand. As countries like China and India have in recent years begun allowing more market transactions to replace government controls, their economies have begun growing much more rapidly.

Growing economies mean rising demand for food, for shelter, for more of the amenities of life. That in turn means a rising demand for oil, leading to rising oil prices around the world.

Those who think in terms of supply and demand suggest— do surprises never end?— we ought to supply more oil to meet the rising demand. But the very politicians who are noisiest about the high price of oil are the most bitterly opposed to increasing the supply.

Drilling for more oil might disturb some animals or birds or fish. Worse yet, on a clear day people with beach front homes might be able to see an offshore oil rig out on the horizon.

Even those who can't see oil being drilled in some isolated hinterland in Alaska would know that the drilling was going on, and that would upset their sensitive natures.

So we are left with nothing we can do about the rising demand for oil around the world, nothing we are willing to do about increasing the supply of oil, and angry denunciations of rising oil prices.

The politically correct answer is that we must have "alternative energy sources" and "conservation." At what cost— in money, in jobs, in constraints on people's lives— is too crass a question for those delicate souls who are dead set against producing more oil.

These souls are apparently not so delicate, however, that they are bothered by the deaths of coal miners who get killed producing one of those "alternative energy sources" that sound so nice when you don't count the costs.

Many of the same delicate sensitivities have kept nuclear power plants or hydroelectric dams from being built in the United States for decades. Some in liberal political or media circles talk ominously about the Three Mile Island nuclear power plant "disaster"— in which no one was killed, as compared to coal mines, in which lives continue to be lost, year after year.

Meanwhile, the fetishes of a self-congratulatory few, who demonize others as selfish, impose staggering costs on the country as a whole. Facts get nowhere against these fetishes because the fetishes are what provide a badge of identity as wonderful and special people.

Photographic Fraud

The media have an obvious vested interest in constantly urging that cameras be allowed in more places where governmental decisions are being made, including the Supreme Court of the United States. Like so many things that are said to be good for the public, this is something that would be good only for its advocates— and harmful to the process of making decisions in the public interest, as distinguished from providing a forum for grandstanding.

The adage that "seeing is believing" should be a warning. What you see in politics is what politicians want you to see. You believe it at your own risk— and at greater risks to the country.

Televised Congressional hearings are not just broadcasts of what happens to be going on in Congress. They are staged events to create a prepackaged impression.

Politically, they are millions of dollars' worth of free advertising for incumbents, while campaign finance laws impede their challengers from being able even to buy name recognition or to present their cases to the public nearly as often.

The real work of Congress gets done where there are no cameras and no microphones— and where politicians can talk turkey with one another to make deals that could not be made with the public listening in.

To be a fly on the wall, able to listen in while these talks were going on, would no doubt be very enlightening, even if painfully disillusioning. But that is not what you are getting in video footage on the evening news.

Some might argue that, in the absence of the cameras, many people might not know what is going on in Congress or in the courts. But being uninformed is not nearly as bad as being misled.

For one thing, it is much easier to know that you are uninformed than to know that you are being misled.

Quite aside from the fraudulence of a photographic facade, even if everyone involved played it straight, there is often remarkably little to be learned from observing a court case, for example, unless you understand the legal framework within which that case is to be decided. That is especially so in appellate courts, including the Supreme Court.

The same thing applies in many other contexts. You could watch televised brain surgery for years without getting a clue, if you had no medical training that would enable you to understand what is being done and why— and what the alternatives are that you do not see on camera, much less know whether the surgeon has consummate skill or is botching the whole thing.

The more complex the issue, the more likely that understanding the context is vastly more important than seeing a picture and hearing sound bites.

Wars are especially susceptible to being distorted on camera. A dramatic event with emotional impact need not tell you what its military significance is. The viewer is able only to react emotionally, in circumstances where rationality can be the difference between life and death, not only for the combatants, but also for the societies from which they come.

Even when televised Congressional hearings are meaningless in themselves— the real decisions having been made off camera— their implications can be devastating. But implications cannot be televised.

Over the past two decades, judicial confirmation hearings have often become exercises in character assassination against nominees that Senators oppose for political reasons having nothing to do with the inflammatory charges that are aired on nationwide TV.

Judges who have for years supported civil rights have been depicted as racists. Other events in their careers have been twisted beyond recognition. Utterly irrelevant questions have been raised to appeal emotionally to uninformed television viewers.

The most direct harm is of course to the nominees. But the most important harm is to the public and to the country. Not only are many top-notch people lost and many innocuous second-raters appointed in their place, many other top-notch people refuse even to be nominated, rather than see the sterling reputation of a lifetime destroyed by political demagogues.

None of those lost people and their talents are televised, though they may be far more important than what is televised.

Political Corruption

The over-riding quest for re-election is at the heart of the corruption of public officials who betray the public trust in order to get the money needed to pay for their political campaigns. It is hard to see how that corruption can be ended, except by ending re-elections with a limit of one term and a ban on running for another office for several years.

That way, the one term can be spent taking care of the duties of the office instead of taking care of promoting a political career in that office or other offices.

There are, of course, other sources of corruption. Members of Congress whose work puts them in the rarefied company of movers and shakers in the private sector, who make ten or a hundred times what Congressmen are paid, may find it tempting to accept perks like free flights on corporate jets or weekends at expensive watering holes. Some may hope for lucrative jobs after leaving politics.

Maybe that won't influence Congressional votes. But maybe it will.

The stakes are too high for us to be penny-wise and pound-foolish by putting trillions of dollars of the taxpayers' money in the hands of elected officials who are paid less than the beginning salary of a top student from a top law school.

If we paid every member of Congress $10 million a year, that would not increase the federal budget by one percent.

Chances are that it would reduce the federal budget considerably, when members of the Senate or the House of Representatives no longer needed campaign contributions or the personal favors of special interest groups and their lobbyists.

One term in the Senate would bring in $60 million, which most people could live on for life, without being beholden to anybody and without having to seek a job afterwards for special interests, much less having to sell their soul to continue a political career.

Money is not the only thing that corrupts. Power also corrupts and some people go into politics for power.

Nothing can be done about such people— except force them to compete with other people, drawn from a far larger pool, including top people in highly paid professions who can seldom afford to serve in Congress today at the expense of their family's standard of living and financial security.

Do we want laws made by people who would sacrifice their families in order to get their hands on the levers of power? Or people who can serve in Congress because they inherited wealth— and therefore have never had to personally experience what ordinary people experience and learn from, including government red tape?

We need laws written by people who have confronted life in the real world, not in the sheltered world of trust fund recipients or the insulated cocoon of academia. Nor do we need people who have nothing to offer in the private sector that would earn them more than what they currently receive in Congress.

Inexperienced power seekers include not only members of Congress but also their staffs, who are often fresh out of academia, with little experience in the real world, many untested notions, and often a touch of vanity as one of the anointed.

The idea of paying the kind of money that would attract the kind of people we need in government runs against many prejudices. Just plain envy is one. Some people feel that those they elect should not make so much more than they do.

But think about it: If your child had some life-threatening condition that required some very demanding surgery, would you worry about whether the surgeon who saves your child's life had an annual income that was several times what you make?

Members of Congress have not only trillions of dollars of our tax money in their hands, they also have in their hands our lives and the lives of our children and our nation. Are you going to worry about their incomes or about what caliber of people we can attract to make the momentous decisions that have to be made?

Yes, it would be nice if all public officials were self-sacrificing individuals who had no other thought than doing their best for their country. It would also be nice if voters watched elected officials 24/7. But the best is the enemy of the good. The road to Utopia has repeatedly turned out to be the road to hell, in countries around the world.

Tragic Implications

Two recent tragedies— in Minnesota and in Utah— have held the nation's attention. The implications of these tragedies also deserve attention.

Those politicians who are always itching to raise tax rates have seized upon the neglected infrastructure of the country as another reason to do what they are always trying to do.

Those who live by talking points now have a great one: "How can we fight an expensive war and repair our neglected infrastructure without raising taxes?"

Plausible as this might sound, tax rates are not tax revenues. The two things have moved in opposite directions too many times, over too many years, for us to take these clever talking points at face value.

The Bush administration is not the first administration in which a reduction in tax rates has been followed by an increase in tax revenues. The same thing happened during the Reagan administration, the Kennedy administration and the Coolidge administration.

Tax rates and tax revenues have moved in opposite directions many times, not only at the federal level, but also at state and local levels, as well as in foreign countries.

How many times does it have to happen before people stop equating tax rates with tax revenues? Do the tax-and-spend politicians and their media supporters not know any better— or are they counting on the rest of us not knowing any better?

Even if we were to assume that higher tax rates will automatically result in significantly higher tax revenues, the case for throwing more money at infrastructure would still be weak.

Some of the money already appropriated for maintaining and repairing infrastructure is being diverted into other pet projects of politicians.

Money supposedly set aside for repairing potholes and maintaining bridges is diverted to the building of bicycle paths or subsidizing ferries or buses. These other things have more of a political pay-off.

Not only are there well-publicized ribbon-cutting ceremonies for building something new, many of these new things can be named for the politicians who had them built. Thus there are all sorts of government structures named for Senator Ted Stevens in Alaska and for Senator Robert Byrd in West Virginia.

But nobody names pothole repairs for anybody or puts any politician's name on the rivets used to repair an existing bridge. Moreover, nobody blames a politician when a bridge collapses years after he put his name on some government building with money that could have been used to make bridges safer longer.

If the collapse occurs on somebody else's watch, it will be somebody else's political problem.

More tax revenue would just allow these same political games to be played with more money. More might be accomplished by forbidding any government facility from being named for anyone who is not already dead.

Maybe then we might get more potholes filled and more rusty rivets replaced on bridges.

The other recent tragedy that has held the nation's painful attention— the mine cave-in in Utah— also has implications that few seem to notice.

We could have far fewer men going down into those mines in the first place if we could use other readily available and economically viable substitutes for coal, such as nuclear power or more of our own oil.

Here too, politics is the problem. The only "alternative energy sources" that are on the political agenda are those few very expensive options that environmentalist zealots approve.

Nuclear power is not on the green zealots' approved list, even though nuclear power is widely used in other countries.

Some say nuclear power is not safe. But nothing is categorically "safe." The only serious question is how its safety compares to that of alternative ways of generating energy.

Ask the families of the trapped miners if they think mining is safe. Ask them if they would rather face the grim reality of a death in their family rather than the hypothetical possibility of inconveniencing some caribou in Alaska.

A Home Invader Program?

People who are pushing for a "guest worker" program show not the slightest interest in what has been happening under guest worker programs in Europe. Facts are apparently irrelevant.

So is logic. Guests are people you invite to your home. Gate crashers are people who come without being invited. Home invaders are people who break in, despite doors that have been shut to keep them out.

If the discussion of immigration laws respected either logic or honesty, we would be talking about a program to legalize home invaders instead of a guest worker program.

As for facts, guest workers from Third World countries have created centers of crime and violence in Europe, and some guest worker communities have become breeding grounds for terrorists.

Just as crime and violence in American inner cities have led not only to "white flight" but also to a flight of the black, Hispanic and Asian middle classes, so in Europe much of the native-born European population has fled from cities like Amsterdam, Rotterdam, and Brussels.

Joel Kotkin's classic book *The City* noted the "influx of immigrants" who were "recruited to Europe during the labor shortages of the 1950s and 1960s" who have become "an increasingly angry and sometimes violent element in what long had been remarkably peaceful urban areas."

Another classic book— *Our Culture, What's Left of It* by Theodore Dalrymple— found a similar pattern in France.

Long before the Muslim riots in Paris which shocked France and the world, Dalrymple pointed out how immigrants in France had become a major source of crime and violence, not only in Paris but in other parts of the country.

The housing projects immediately surrounding Paris have become concentrations of "several million" Third World immigrants— a population filled with "the hatred it bears for the other, 'official' society of France."

They are not appeased by "the people who carelessly toss them the crumbs of Western prosperity." What they want is what most people want— respect— and this cannot be given to them, least of all by the French welfare state.

In order to feel self-respect, the young especially "needed to see themselves as warriors in a civil war, not mere ne'er-do-wells and criminals."

This anti-social vision has been supported and even celebrated by many intellectuals, much as both black and white intellectuals have celebrated the senseless brutality and cheap vulgarity of rap music in America.

What may be especially relevant to the situation in the United States is that the immigrant parents and grandparents of the violent youths came to France with a very different view.

They were glad to be in France, which for most was a big improvement over where they came from. "They were better Frenchmen than either their children or grandchildren," Dalrymple noted.

They would never have booed the French national anthem at a public event, as the later generations did— and as the American national anthem has been booed in Los Angeles.

The later generations were not born in the Third World countries from which their parents and grandparents escaped. They were born in France, and resented not having the same prosperity as other Frenchmen.

Here again, the media and the intelligentsia in France, as in the United States, tend to turn differences in achievement— "gaps," "disparities"— into social injustices rather than reflections of differences in the things that create achievement.

One of the things that make many people such passionate advocates of amnesty for illegal immigrants from Mexico is that so many Mexican immigrants are hard-working, decent family people.

That was also true of many Third World "guest workers" in Europe, who were glad to be there, but whose children and grandchildren have developed very different and very poisonous attitudes— with the help of activists, demagogues, and the media.

Today's illegal immigrants are too often analogized to early 20th century immigrants from Europe. But their situation is far more similar to that of contemporary "guest workers" in Europe.

An Ugly Reality

Thank heaven for the massive marches across the country by those favoring illegal immigrants. These marches revealed the ugly truth behind the fog of pious words and clever political spin from the media and from both Democrats and Republicans in Washington.

"Guest workers"? Did any of the strident speakers, with their in-your-face bombast in Spanish, sound like guests? Did they sound like people who wanted to become Americans?

Were they even asking for amnesty? They didn't sound like they were asking for anything. They sounded like they were telling. Demanding. Threatening.

Somebody must have told them that their Mexican flags that dominated the earlier marches were not making a good impression on television, so they started flying American flags. But such cosmetic changes did not keep the ugly reality from coming through in their hostile speeches.

These were not the speeches of people who wanted to join American society but people who wanted their own turf on American soil— in disregard and defiance of what American citizens want.

Europe has already been through this "guest worker" policy that we are being urged to follow. They have learned the hard way what it means to have a growing foreign population in their midst— a population that insists on remaining foreign and hostile to the culture, values and people around them.

Some European countries have learned this lesson at the cost of riots and bloodshed in the streets and lives lost in terrorist attacks. Others have only had to contend with national polarization— thus far— but polarization is not a small thing.

In this country, however, there are still people who refuse to learn any lesson at all. Some business interests see only an opportunity to get cheap labor. Some intellectuals see only abstract principles about abstract people crossing an abstract border.

Some tell us loftily that earlier generations of immigrants who were once thought to be unassimilable turned out over time to become as American as anyone else and patriotic citizens.

That might well be true of immigrants from Mexico, both legal and illegal, if the circumstances of today were the same as the circumstances during an earlier era of immigration from Europe. But circumstances are not the same— and those circumstances are not going to become the same by pretending that they are.

The ugly display of grievance-mongering bombast at the illegal immigrant marches is just one of those circumstances that are not the same as in an earlier era.

When people came here from Europe, they came here to become Americans. There was no prouder title for them.

American generals of German ancestry led the fight against Germany in both World Wars. The Irish "Fighting 69th" earned its fame on the battlefields of the First World War and Japanese American fighting units were among the most highly decorated in World War II. They proved they were Americans.

The underlying tragedy of the present situation is that it is doubtful whether the activist loudmouths, who were too contemptuous of this country to even speak its language while demanding its benefits, represent most immigrants from Mexico.

Both legal and illegal immigrants have come here primarily to work and make a better life for themselves and their families. But a country requires more than workers. It requires people who are citizens not only in name but in commitment.

Americanization did not happen automatically in earlier times and it will not happen automatically today. Immigrants in an earlier era had leaders and organizations actively working to transform them into Americans— the Catholic Church with the Irish and numerous organizations among the Jews, for example.

Today's immigrant activists and the politicians who kowtow to them have just the opposite agenda, to keep foreigners foreign and to make other Americans accept and adjust to that. It will be a national tragedy if they succeed.

Just what problem will amnesty solve? Illegal aliens will benefit and politicians will benefit by sweeping the illegality under the rug by making it legal. But how will American citizens benefit? America can lose big time.

Fables for Adults

M any years ago, as a small child, I was told one of those old-fashioned fables for children. It was about a dog with a bone in his mouth, who was walking on a log across a stream.

The dog looked down into the water and saw his reflection. He thought it was another dog with a bone in his mouth— and it seemed to him that the other dog's bone was bigger than his. He decided that he was going to take the other dog's bone away and opened his mouth to attack. The result was that his own bone fell into the water and was lost.

At the time, I didn't like that story and wished they hadn't told it to me. But the passing years and decades have made me realize how important that story was, because it was not really about dogs but about people.

Today we are living in a time when the President of the United States is telling us that he is going to help us take that other dog's bone away— and the end result is likely to be very much like what it was in that children's fable.

Whether we are supposed to take that bone away from the doctors, the hospitals, the pharmaceutical companies or the insurance companies, the net result is likely to be the same— most of us will end up with worse medical care than we have available today. We will have opened our mouth and dropped a very big bone into the water.

While I was told a story in my childhood to help me understand something about the real world, today adults are being told things to reduce them to childish thinking.

The most childish of all the things being said in the august setting of a joint session of Congress last week was that millions of people can be added to the government's health insurance plan without increasing the federal deficit at all.

If the President of the United States could do that, it is hard to imagine what he would do as an encore. Walking on water would be an anticlimax.

What is equally childish is the notion that the great majority of Americans who have medical insurance, and who say they are satisfied with it, should be panicked and stampeded into supporting vast increases in the arbitrary power of Washington bureaucrats to take medical decisions out of the hands of their doctors— all ostensibly because a minority of Americans do not have medical insurance.

There was a time, within living memory, when most Americans did not have health insurance— and it was not the end of the world, as so many in politics and the media seem to be depicting it today.

As someone who lived through that era, and who spent decades without medical insurance, I find it hard to be panicked and stampeded into bigger and worse problems because some people do not have medical insurance, including many who could afford it if they chose to.

What did we do, back during the years when most Americans had no medical insurance? I did what most people did. I depended on a "single payer"— myself. When I didn't have the money, I paid off my medical bills in installments.

The birth of my first child was not covered by medical insurance. I paid off the bill, month by month, until the time finally came when I could tell my wife that the baby was now ours, free and clear.

In a country where everything imaginable is bought and paid for on credit, why is it suddenly a national crisis if some people cannot pay cash up front for medical treatment?

That is not the best way to do things for all people and all medical treatments, which is why most Americans today choose to have medical insurance. But millions of other people choose not to— often young and healthy people, sometimes deadbeats who use emergency rooms and don't pay at all.

Is this ideal? No. But if every deviation from the ideal is a reason to be panicked and stampeded into putting dangerous arbitrary powers into the hands of government, then go directly to totalitarianism, do not pass "Go", do not collect $200.

And go ahead and drop your bone in the water, in hopes that you can get somebody else's bigger bone.

ECONOMIC ISSUES

E conomics was long ago called "the dismal science," and for a very good reason. It poured cold water on all sorts of wonderful-sounding ideas.

Economics and politics deal with the same fundamental problem: What everyone wants always adds up to more than there is. Economics can give no solution to that problem, and can at best offer various ways that trade-offs may be made, in order to try to optimize the inherently limited possibilities. But politics offers solutions every day— however illusory, counterproductive or even disastrous those solutions may turn out to be. In the short run, which is when elections are held, politicians are a lot more popular than economists.

Most of the graduates of even our most prestigious universities leave these illustrious campuses utterly ignorant of economics. Even distinguished professors in other fields are often not only ignorant, but misinformed, about the most basic principles of economics. Harvard's eminent historian, Professor Arthur M. Schlesinger, Jr., admitted that he had no real interest in economics, though that did not stop him from concluding that President Franklin D. Roosevelt's administration saved the American economy during the Great Depression of the 1930s.

We are all necessarily ignorant of vast fields of human endeavor, not only nuclear physics but even the production of yogurt. However, we have the option of not presuming to reach conclusions about such things. But virtually every public official we vote for is going to have an impact on the economy, for better or worse. We cannot, like Pontius Pilate, simply wash our hands. We can only be informed or ignorant or— worst of all— misinformed.

Some of the ways and consequences of being misinformed are explored in the essays that follow.

Tax Cuts and "Trickle Down"

The *New York Times* of May 21, 2006 featured estimates of how much revenue the federal government is losing as a result of tax cuts, more than $50 billion over a five-year period. Meanwhile, a front-page story in the *Wall Street Journal* reported the government as receiving "a surge in unanticipated revenue coming from the rich."

There is no contradiction between these two stories. The *Times* reported estimates, while the *Wall Street Journal* reported what actually happened. Moreover, there is no real difference in outlook between the writers who wrote these two stories.

To the *Wall Street Journal* writer, the increased tax revenue from "the rich" was "a windfall for the U.S. Treasury."

There has long been a difference in outlook between the reporters who write up the news for the *Wall Street Journal* and those who write the same newspaper's editorial page. If the reporter thinks that the increased revenue to the Treasury was "unanticipated," that suggests that she has not been reading the editorial pages of her own newspaper.

For years— indeed, decades— the *Wall Street Journal*'s editorial page has repeatedly been arguing that cutting tax rates increases tax revenues. Nor did this idea originate with them. There is a whole school of economists who have been saying the same thing even longer.

There is nothing "unanticipated" about the increased revenue. It was unanticipated by the Congressional Budget Office's estimates, but that is why the CBO has come under fire from economists. But apparently none of this has yet registered on the *Wall Street Journal's* front page reporter.

More than 40 years ago, President John F. Kennedy got Congress to cut tax rates, with the idea that this would provide incentives to change economic behavior in a way that would increase economic growth and individual incomes, and therefore lead to even more tax revenue coming into the Treasury than had been the case under the higher tax rates. That is exactly what happened.

Years later, Ronald Reagan made the same argument and his "tax cuts for the rich" produced the same result. Tax receipts during every year of the 1980s were higher than they had ever been in any year before. Moreover, taxes paid specifically by "the rich" were higher than before, because their incomes rose so much as the economy boomed that they paid more total taxes despite the reduced tax rate.

How surprised should we be that exactly the same thing has happened after tax cuts under the Bush administration? Apparently very surprised if we were front-page reporters for the *Wall Street Journal.*

Given the steeply "progressive" tax rates, most of the taxes paid are paid by people in income brackets that liberals choose to call "the rich," though that label would probably come as some surprise to many people in those brackets. Therefore any serious reductions in tax rates will necessarily directly affect them most.

The point, however, is not simply to move money around but to change behavior in a way that will result in more economic activity. Tax cuts have a long track record of doing that, resulting in rising national incomes and rising employment.

But there is no way that some people are ever going to admit that what they call "tax cuts for the rich" are tax cuts for the economy. As far as they are concerned, this is all just an excuse to "give" something to the rich, in hopes that it will "trickle down" to the lower income brackets.

A year ago, this column defied anyone to quote any economist— in government, academia, or anywhere else outside an insane asylum— who had ever argued in favor of such a "trickle down theory."

Many people quoted David Stockman as saying that others had made that argument. But David Stockman was not even among the first thousand people to make that claim. What is crucial is that not one of those who made the claim could provide a single quote from anybody who had advocated a "trickle-down theory."

The "trickle down theory" has been a stock phrase on the left for decades and yet not one of those who denounce it can find anybody who advocated it. The tenacity with which they cling to these catchwords shows how desperately they need them, if only to safeguard their vision of the world and of themselves.

Income Confusion

Anyone who follows the media has probably heard many times that the rich are getting richer, the poor are getting poorer, and incomes of the population in general are stagnating. Moreover, those who say such things can produce many statistics, including data from the Census Bureau, which seem to indicate that.

On the other hand, income tax data recently released by the Internal Revenue Service seem to show the exact opposite: People in the bottom fifth of income-tax filers in 1996 had their incomes increase by 91 percent by 2005.

The top one percent— "the rich" who are supposed to be monopolizing the money, according to the left— saw their incomes decline by a whopping 26 percent.

Meanwhile, the average taxpayers' real income increased by 24 percent between 1996 and 2005.

How can all this be? How can official statistics from different agencies of the same government— the Census Bureau and the IRS— lead to such radically different conclusions?

There are wild cards in such data that need to be kept in mind when you hear income statistics thrown around— especially when they are thrown around by people who are trying to prove something for political purposes.

One of these wild cards is that most Americans do not stay in the same income brackets throughout their lives. Millions of people move from one bracket to another in just a few years.

What that means statistically is that comparing the top income bracket with the bottom income bracket over a period of years tells you nothing about what is happening to the actual flesh-and-blood human beings who are moving between brackets during those years.

That is why the IRS data, which are for people 25 years old and older, and which follow the same individuals over time, find those in the bottom 20 percent of income-tax filers almost doubling their income in a decade. That is why they are no longer in the same bracket.

That is also why the share of income going to the bottom 20 percent bracket can be going down, as the Census Bureau data show, while the income going to the people who began the decade in that bracket is going up by large amounts.

Unfortunately, most income statistics, including those from the Census Bureau, do not follow individuals over time. The Internal Revenue Service does that and so does a study at the University of Michigan, but they are the exceptions rather than the rule.

Following trends among income brackets over the years creates the illusion of following people over time. But the only way to follow people is to follow people.

Another wild card in income statistics is that many such statistics are about households or families—whose sizes vary over time, vary between one racial or ethnic group and another, and vary between one income bracket and another.

That is why household or family income can remain virtually unchanged for decades while per capita income is going up by very large amounts. The number of people per household and per family is declining.

Differences in the number of people per household from one ethnic group to another is why Hispanics have higher household incomes than blacks, while blacks have higher individual incomes than Hispanics.

Considering the millions of dollars being paid to each of the anchors who broadcast network news, surely these networks can afford to hire a few statisticians to check the statistics being thrown around, before these numbers are broadcast across the land as facts on which we are supposed to base policies and elect presidents.

Now that the Internal Revenue Service data show the opposite of what the media and the politicians have been saying for years, should we expect either to change? Not bloody likely.

The University of Michigan study, which has been going on for decades, shows patterns very similar to those of the IRS data. Those patterns have been ignored for decades.

Too many in the media and in politics choose whatever statistics fit their preconceptions.

Upside Down Economics

From television specials to newspaper editorials, the media are pushing the idea that current economic problems were caused by the market and that only the government can rescue us.

What was lacking in the housing market, they say, was government regulation of the market's "greed." That makes great moral melodrama, but it turns the facts upside down.

It was precisely government intervention which turned a thriving industry into a basket case.

An economist specializing in financial markets gave a glimpse of the history of housing markets when he said: "Lending money to American homebuyers had been one of the least risky and most profitable businesses a bank could engage in for nearly a century."

That was what the market was like before the government intervened. Like many government interventions, it began small and later grew.

The Community Reinvestment Act of 1977 directed federal regulatory agencies to "encourage" banks and other lending institutions "to help meet the credit needs of the local communities in which they are chartered consistent with the safe and sound operation of such institutions."

That sounds pretty innocent and, in fact, it had little effect for more than a decade. However, its premise was that bureaucrats and politicians know where loans should go, better than people who are in the business of making loans.

The real potential of that premise became apparent in the 1990s, when the Department of Housing and Urban Development (HUD) imposed a requirement that mortgage lenders demonstrate with hard data that they were meeting their responsibilities under the Community Reinvestment Act.

What HUD wanted were numbers showing that mortgage loans were being made to low-income and moderate-income people on a scale that HUD expected, even if this required "innovative or flexible" mortgage eligibility standards.

In other words, quotas were imposed— and if some people didn't meet the standards, then the standards needed to be changed.

Both HUD and the Department of Justice began bringing lawsuits against mortgage bankers when a higher percentage of minority applicants than white applicants were turned down for mortgage loans.

A substantial majority of both black and white mortgage loan applicants had their loans approved but a statistical difference was enough to get a bank sued.

It should also be noted that the same statistical sources from which data on blacks and whites were obtained usually contained data on Asian Americans as well. But those data on Asian Americans were almost never mentioned.

Whites were turned down for mortgage loans more often than Asian Americans. But saying that would undermine the reasoning on which the whole moral melodrama and political crusades were based.

Lawsuits were only part of the pressures put on lenders by government officials. Banks and other lenders are overseen by regulatory agencies and must go to those agencies for approval of many business decisions that other businesses make without needing anyone else's approval.

Government regulators refused to approve such decisions when a lender was under investigation for not producing satisfactory statistics on loans to low-income people or minorities.

Under growing pressures from both the Clinton administration and later the George W. Bush administration, banks began to lower their lending standards.

Mortgage loans with no down payment, no income verification and other "creative" financial arrangements abounded. Although this was done under pressures begun in the name of the poor and minorities, people who were neither could also get these mortgage loans.

With mortgage loans widely available to people with questionable prospects of being able to keep up the payments, it was an open invitation to financial disaster.

Those who warned of the dangers had their warnings dismissed. Now, apparently, we need more politicians intervening in more industries, if you believe the politicians and the media.

An Economic Whodunit

During bad times, the blame game is the biggest game in Washington. Wall Street "greed" or "predatory" lenders seem to be favorite targets to blame for our current economic woes.

When government policy is mentioned at all in handing out blame, it is usually blamed for not imposing enough regulation on the private sector. But there is still the question whether any of these explanations can stand up under scrutiny.

Take Wall Street "greed." Is there any evidence that people in Wall Street were any less interested in making money during all the decades and generations when investments in housing were among the safest investments around? If their greed did not bring on an economic disaster before, why would it bring it on now?

As for lenders, how could they have expected to satisfy their greed by lending to people who were not likely to repay them?

The one agency of government that is widely blamed is the Federal Reserve System— which still keeps the heat away from elected politicians. Nor is the Fed completely blameless. It kept interest rates extremely low for years. That undoubtedly contributed to an increased demand for housing, since lower interest rates mean lower monthly mortgage payments.

But an increased demand for housing does not automatically mean higher housing prices. In places where supply is free to rise to meet demand, such as Manhattan in the 1950s or Las Vegas in the 1980s, increased demand simply led to more housing units being built, without an increase in real prices— that is, money prices adjusted for inflation.

What led to a boom in housing prices was increased demand in places where supply was artificially restricted. Coastal California was the largest of these places where severe legal restrictions on building houses led to skyrocketing housing prices. Just between 2000 and 2005, for example, home prices more than doubled in Los Angeles and San Diego, in response to rising demand in places where supply was not allowed to rise to meet it.

At the height of the housing boom in 2005, the ten areas with the biggest home price increases over the previous five years were all in California. That year, the average home price in California was more than half a million dollars, even though the average size of the homes sold was just 1,600 square feet.

Although California— and especially coastal California— was the biggest place with skyrocketing housing prices, it was not the only place. Other enclaves, here and there, with severe housing restrictions also had rapidly rising housing prices to levels far above the national average.

If the housing boom was so localized, how did this become a national problem? Because the money that financed housing in areas with housing price booms was supplied by financial institutions across the country and even across the ocean.

Mortgages made in California were sold to nationwide financial institutions, including Fannie Mae and Freddie Mac, and to firms in Wall Street which bundled thousands of these mortgages into financial securities that were sold nationally and internationally.

The problem was that, not only were these mortgages based on housing prices inflated by the Federal Reserve's low-interest rate policies, many of the home buyers had been granted mortgages under federal government pressures on lenders to lend to people who would not ordinarily qualify, whether because of low income, bad credit history or other factors likely to make them bigger credit risks.

This was not something that federal regulatory agencies permitted. It was something that federal regulatory agencies— under pressure from politicians— pressured and threatened lenders into doing in the name of "affordable housing."

The housing market collapse was set off when the Federal Reserve returned interest rates to more normal levels, but it was a financial house of cards that was due to collapse, sending shock waves through the economy. It was just a matter of when, not if.

A fuller account of all this appeared last year in my book *The Housing Boom and Bust*. The revised and expanded edition shows how more of the same kinds of policies today are making it harder for the economy to recover. It's not that politicians never learn. They learn how much they can get away with, when they can blame others.

False Solutions and Real Problems

S omeone once said that Senator Hubert Humphrey, liberal icon of an earlier generation, had more solutions than there were problems.

Senator Humphrey was not unique in that respect. In fact, our present economic crisis has developed out of politicians providing solutions to problems that did not exist— and, as a result, producing a problem whose existence is all too real and all too painful.

What was the problem that didn't exist? It was a national problem of unaffordable housing. The political crusade for affordable housing got into high gear in the 1990s and led to all kinds of changes in mortgage lending practices, which in turn led to a housing boom and bust that has left us in the mess we are now trying to dig out of.

Usually housing affordability is measured in terms of how much of the average person's income it takes to cover either apartment rent or a monthly mortgage payment.

There were certainly places here and there where it took half a family's income just to put a roof over their heads. Many such places were in coastal California but there were a few others, here and there, on the east coast and elsewhere.

But vast areas of the country in between— "flyover country" to the east coast and west coast elites— had housing prices that took no larger share of the average American's income than in the decade before the affordable housing crusade got under way.

Why then a national crusade by Washington politicians over local problems? Probably as good an answer as any is that "It seemed like a good idea at the time." How are we to be kept aware of how compassionate and how important our elected officials are unless they are busy solving some problem for us?

The problem of skyrocketing housing prices was all too real in those places where this problem existed. When you have to live on half your income because the other half goes for housing, that's a real downer.

Almost invariably, these severe local problems had local causes— usually severe local restrictions on building homes. These restrictions had a variety of politically attractive names, ranging from "open space" laws and "smart growth" policies to "environmental protection" and "farmland preservation."

Like most wonderful-sounding political slogans, none of these lofty goals was discussed in terms of that one four-letter word that people do not use in polite political society— "cost."

No one asked how many hundreds of thousands of dollars would be added to the cost of an average home by "open space" laws, for example. Yet empirical studies have shown that land-use restrictions added at least a hundred thousand dollars to the average home price in dozens of places around the country.

In some places, such as coastal California, these restrictions added several hundred thousand dollars to the price of the average home.

In other words, where the problem was real, local politicians were the cause. National politicians then tried to depict this as a national problem that they would solve.

How would they solve it? By pressuring banks and other lenders to lower their requirements for making mortgage loans, so that more people could buy houses. The Department of Housing and Urban Development gave the government-sponsored enterprise Fannie Mae quotas for how many mortgages it should buy that were made out for people with low to moderate incomes.

Like most political "solutions," the solution to the affordable housing "problem" took little or no account of the wider repercussions this would entail.

Various economists and others warned repeatedly that lowered lending standards meant more risky mortgages. Given the complex relationships among banks and other financial institutions, including many big Wall Street firms, if mortgages started defaulting, all the financial dominoes could start falling.

These warnings were brushed aside. Politicians were too busy solving a national problem that didn't exist. In the process, they created very real problems. Now they are offering even more solutions that will undoubtedly lead to even bigger problems.

Curing Poverty or Using Poverty?

"China is lifting a million people a month out of poverty." It is just one statement in an interesting new book titled *The Undercover Economist* by Tim Harford. But it has huge implications.

I haven't checked out the statistics but they sound reasonable. If so, this is something worth everyone's attention.

People on the political left make a lot of noise about poverty and advocate all sorts of programs and policies to reduce it but they show incredibly little interest in how poverty has actually been reduced, whether in China or anywhere else.

You can bet the rent money that the left will show little or no interest in how Chinese by the millions are rising out of poverty every year. The left showed far more interest in China back when it was run by Mao in far left fashion— and when millions of Chinese were starving.

Those of us who are not on the left ought to take a closer look at today's Chinese rising out of poverty.

First of all, what does it even mean to say that "China is lifting a million people a month out of poverty"? Where would the Chinese government get the money to do that?

The only people the Chinese government can tax are mainly the people in China. A country can't lift itself up by its own bootstraps that way. Nor has there ever been enough foreign aid to lift a million people a month out of poverty.

If the Chinese government hasn't done it, then who has? The Chinese people. They did not rise out of poverty by receiving largess from anybody.

The only thing that can cure poverty is wealth. The Chinese acquired wealth the old-fashioned way: They created it.

After the death of Mao, government controls over the market began to be relaxed— first tentatively, in selected places and for selected industries. Then, as those places and those industries began to prosper dramatically, similar relaxations of government control took place elsewhere, with similar results.

Even foreigners were allowed to come in and invest in China and sell their goods in China. But this was not just a transfer of wealth.

Foreigners did not come in to help the Chinese but to help themselves. The only way they could benefit, and the Chinese benefit at the same time, was if more total wealth was created. That is what happened but the political left has virtually no interest in the creation of wealth, in China or anywhere else, despite all of their proclaimed concern for "the poor."

Since wealth is the only thing that can cure poverty, you might think that the left would be as obsessed with the creation of wealth as they are with the redistribution of wealth. But you would be wrong.

When it comes to lifting people out of poverty, redistribution of income and wealth has a much poorer and more spotty track record than the creation of wealth. In some places, such as Zimbabwe today, attempts at a redistribution of wealth have turned out to be a redistribution of poverty.

While the creation of wealth may be more effective for enabling millions of people to rise out of poverty, it provides no special role for the political left, no puffed up importance, no moral superiority, no power for them to wield over others. Redistribution is clearly better for the left.

Leftist emphasis on "the poor" proceeds as if the poor were some separate group. But, in most Western countries, at least, millions of people who are "poor" at one period of their lives are "rich" at another period of their lives— as these terms are conventionally defined.

How can that be? People tend to become more productive— create more wealth— over time, with more experience and an accumulation of skills and training.

That is reflected in incomes that are two or three times higher in later years than at the beginning of a career. But that too is of little or no interest to the political left.

Things that work for millions of people offer little to the left, and ultimately the left is about the left, not about the people they claim to want to lift out of poverty.

The "Greed" Fallacy

I n an era when our media and even our education system exalt emotions, while ignoring facts and logic, perhaps we should not be surprised that so many people explain economics by "greed."

Today there are adults— including educated adults— who explain multimillion-dollar corporate executives' salaries as being due to "greed."

Think about it: I could become so greedy that I wanted a fortune twice the size of Bill Gates'— but this greed would not increase my income by one cent.

If you want to explain why some people have astronomical incomes, it cannot be simply because of their own desires— whether "greedy" or not— but because of what other people are willing to pay them.

The real question, then, is: Why do other people choose to pay corporate executives so much?

One popular explanation is that executive salaries are set by boards of directors who are spending the stockholders' money and do not care that they are overpaying a CEO, who may be the one responsible for putting them on the board of directors in the first place.

It makes a neat picture and may even be true in some cases. What deals a body blow to this theory, however, is that CEO compensation is even higher in corporations owned by a few giant investment firms, as distinguished from corporations owned by thousands of individual stockholders.

In other words, it is precisely where people are spending their own money and have financial expertise that they bid highest for CEOs. It is precisely where people most fully understand the difference that the right CEO can make in a corporation's profitability that they are willing to bid what it takes to get the executive they want.

If people who are capable of being outstanding executives were a dime a dozen, nobody would pay eleven cents a dozen for them.

Many observers who say that they cannot understand how anyone can be worth $100 million a year do not realize that it is not necessary that they understand it, since it is not their money.

All of us have thousands of things happening around us that we do not understand. We use computers all the time but most of us could not build a computer if our life depended on it— and those few individuals who could probably couldn't grow orchids or train horses.

In short, we all have grossly inadequate knowledge in other people's specialties.

The idea that everything must "justify itself before the bar of reason" goes back at least as far as the 18th century. But that just makes it a candidate for the longest-running fallacy in the world.

Given the high degree of specialization in a modern economy, demanding that everything "justify itself before the bar of reason" means demanding that people who know what they are doing must be subject to the veto of people who don't have a clue about the decisions that they are second-guessing.

It means demanding that ignorance override knowledge.

The ignorant are not just some separate group of people. As Will Rogers said, everybody is ignorant, but just about different things.

Should computer experts tell brain surgeons how to do their job? Or horse trainers tell either of them what to do?

One of the reasons why central planning sounds so good, but has failed so badly that even socialist and communist governments finally abandoned the idea by the end of the 20th century, is that nobody knows enough to second guess everybody else.

Every time oil prices shoot up, there are cries of "greed" and demands by politicians for an investigation of collusion by Big Oil. There have been more than a dozen investigations of oil companies over the years, and none of them has turned up the collusion that is supposed to be responsible for high gas prices.

Now that oil prices have dropped big time, does that mean that oil companies have lost their "greed"? Or could it all be supply and demand— a cause and effect explanation that seems to be harder for some people to understand than emotions like "greed"?

Payday Loans

Words are not the only things that enable political rhetoric to magically transform reality. Numbers can be used just as creatively— and many voters are even more gullible about statistics than they are about words, apparently because statistics seem more objective.

The latest Congressional crusade is to clamp down on small finance companies that provide "payday loans" and check-cashing services in many low-income neighborhoods where there are few banks.

A common practice in making small loans of a few hundred dollars for a few weeks is to charge about $15 per hundred dollars lent. Politicians, the media, community activists and miscellaneous other busybodies are able to transform these numbers into annual percentage charges of several hundred percent, thereby creating moral melodramas and demands that the government "do something" about such "abuses."

Of course, these loans are seldom borrowed for a year. They are often loans for a couple of weeks or less, to meet some difficulty of the moment by people who live from payday to payday, whether they are being paid by a job or are receiving checks from Social Security, unemployment compensation or welfare.

The alternative to getting a payday loan may be having the electricity cut off or not having money to buy some medication. It is worse to borrow from illegal loan sharks, who have their own methods of collecting.

While $15 per hundred dollars may sound like a high rate of interest, it is not all interest. The finance company incurs costs just to process a loan, and these costs are a higher proportion of the total cost for a small loan than for a large loan.

When Oregon imposed a limit of 36 percent annual interest on what a finance company could charge, that meant charging less than $1.50 for a hundred dollar loan for a couple of weeks. A dollar and a half would probably not even cover the cost of processing the loan, much less the risks of default.

Not surprisingly, most of the small finance companies making payday loans in Oregon went out of business. But there are no statistics on how many low-income people turned to loan sharks or had their electricity cut off or had to do without their medicine.

This is just one of the many ways in which self-righteous busybodies leave havoc in their wake, while going away feeling noble.

Statistics played a key role in creating the housing boom and bust that led to the current economic crisis. Back in the 1990s, politicians, the media, community activists like Jesse Jackson and others all made a lot of noise about statistical studies showing that (1) non-whites had lower rates of home-ownership than whites, (2) were turned down for mortgage loans more often than whites, and (3) resorted to more expensive subprime mortgage loans than whites.

All this led to pressures and even quotas for banks to lend to more low-income and minority applicants. That in turn led to lower mortgage lending standards, more risky mortgages, higher default rates and the collapse of financial institutions that bought these more risky mortgages or securities based on them.

We have seen and heard the same kinds of things when statistics about other racial differences have been cited in the same strident voices when other statistics showed blacks laid off more than whites during economic downturns or the children of black women having higher infant mortality rates than the children of white women.

What we have very seldom seen or heard in such parading of statistics are other statistics— which are readily available— showing that (1) whites are turned down for mortgage loans more often than Asian Americans, (2) whites resort to subprime loans more often than Asian Americans, (3) whites have been laid off more in a downturn than Asian Americans, and (4) the children of white mothers have higher infant mortality rates than the children of mothers of Filipino or Mexican ancestry, even though these mothers receive less prenatal care than white mothers.

In other words, numbers do not "speak for themselves." Politicians, the media and others speak for them— very loudly, very cleverly and often very wrongly.

Stimulus or Sedative?

Abraham Lincoln once asked an audience how many legs a dog has, if you called the tail a leg? When the audience said "five," Lincoln corrected them, saying that the answer was four. "The fact that you call a tail a leg does not make it a leg."

That same principle applies today. The fact that politicians call something a "stimulus" does not make it a stimulus. The fact that they call something a "jobs bill" does not mean there will be more jobs.

What have been the actual consequences of all the hundreds of billions of dollars that the government has spent? The idea behind the spending is that it will cause investors to invest, lenders to lend and employers to employ.

That was called "pump priming." To get a pump going, people put a little water into it, so that the pump will then pump out a lot of water. In other words, government money alone was never supposed to restore the economy by itself. It was supposed to get the private sector spending, lending, investing and employing.

The question is: Is that what has actually happened?

The stimulus spending started back in 2008, during the Bush administration, and has continued under the Obama administration, so it has had plenty of time to show what it can do.

After the Bush administration's stimulus spending in 2008, business spending on equipment and software fell— not rose— by 28 percent. Spending on durable goods fell 22 percent.

What about the banks? Four months after the Trouble Asset Relief Program (TARP) poured billions of dollars into the banks, the biggest recipients of that money made 23 percent fewer loans than before. A year later, the credit extended by American banks as a whole was down— not up— by more than $20 billion.

Spending in general was down. The velocity of circulation of money fell faster than it had in half a century.

Just two weeks ago, the *Wall Street Journal* reported, "U.S. banks posted last year their sharpest decline in lending since 1942." You can call it a stimulus, if you want to, just as you can call a tail a leg. But the actual effect of what is called a "stimulus" has been more like that of a sedative.

Why aren't the banks lending, with all that money sitting there gathering dust?

You don't lend when politicians are making it more doubtful whether you are going to get your money back— either on time or at all. From the White House to Capitol Hill, politicians are coming up with all sorts of bright ideas for borrowers not to have to pay back what they borrowed and for lenders not to be able to foreclose on people who are months behind on their mortgage payments.

President Obama keeps telling us that he is "creating jobs." But more and more Americans have no jobs. The unemployment rate has declined slightly, but only because many people have stopped looking for jobs. You are only counted as unemployed if you are still looking for a job.

If all the unemployed people were to decide that it is hopeless and stop looking for work, the unemployment statistics would drop like a rock. But that would hardly be a solution.

What is going on, that nothing seems to work?

None of this is new. What is going on is what went on during the Great Depression of the 1930s. Money circulated more slowly during the 1930s than during the 1920s. Banks lent out a smaller proportion of the money they had on hand during the 1930s than they did in the 1920s. Anti-business ideas and anti-business rhetoric did not create business confidence then, any more than it does now. Economists have estimated that the New Deal prolonged the depression by several years.

This is not another Great Depression, at least not yet, and the economy may recover on its own, if the government will let it. But Obama today, like FDR in the 1930s, cannot leave the economy alone. Both have felt a need to come up with one bright idea after another, to "do something."

The theory is that, if one thing doesn't work, it is just a matter of trying another. But, in an atmosphere where nobody knows what the federal government is going to come up with next, people tend to hang on to their money until they have some idea of what the rules of the game are going to be.

French Student Riots

Student riots in Paris remind us that education at elite academic institutions is not enough to teach either higher morals or basic economics. Not on their side of the Atlantic or on ours.

Why are students at the Sorbonne and other distinguished institutions out trashing the streets and attacking the police? Because they want privileges in the name of rights, and are too ignorant of economics to realize that those privileges cost them jobs.

Like some other European Union countries, France has laws making it hard to fire anybody. The political left has long believed that such laws are a way of reducing unemployment.

More important, they have long remained oblivious to the fact that countries with such laws, such as France and Germany, usually have higher unemployment rates than countries without such laws, such as the United States.

Belatedly, some French officials have begun to see that job security laws make it more risky and costly for an employer to hire inexperienced workers with no track record, whom they would have a hard time getting rid of if they don't work out. The unemployment rate in France is 23 percent for workers who are 25 years old and younger.

To try to deal with this high unemployment rate among young workers, the job security laws have recently been modified to make it easier for employers to fire those workers who are on their first job.

That is what has French students outraged and rampaging through the streets of Paris. They don't want employers to be able to fire them after they graduate and go to work.

Students and their political supporters, including labor unions, depict them as victims. Among the slogans chanted by the rioters is "We're not young flesh for the boss." The fact that many bosses don't seem to want to hire their young flesh seems to be lost on them.

A leftist deputy has declared: "To create discrimination based on age transgresses fundamental rights!"

In other words, people have a right for other people to have to continue employing them, whether those other people want to or not. The "fundamental right" to a job over-rides the rights of other people when they are called "bosses."

The fact that many students can think only in terms of "rights," but not in terms of consequences, shows a major deficiency in their education. The right to a job is obviously not the same thing as a job. Otherwise there would not be a 23 percent unemployment rate among young French workers.

The law can create equal rights for inexperienced young workers and for older workers with a proven track record but the law cannot make them equally productive on the job or equally risky to hire. Nor is rioting likely to make employers any more likely to want young workers working for them.

Estimates of the damage done by the rioters— called "protesters" or "demonstrators" in the mealy-mouthed media— range from hundreds of thousands of dollars to over a million dollars, thus far. They have also shut down dozens of universities, including the Sorbonne, denying an education to other students.

The heady notion of "rights"— and especially the notion that your rights over-ride other people's rights, when those other people belong to some suspect class called "bosses"— is an all too familiar feature of modern welfare state notions.

French Prime Minister Dominique de Villepin, who supports the new labor law, has seen his approval rating drop to 36 percent. That is what happens when you try to talk sense to people who prefer to believe nonsense.

It is elementary economics that adding to the costs, including risks, of hiring workers tends to reduce the number of workers hired. It should not be news to anyone, whether or not they have gone to a university, that raising costs usually results in fewer transactions.

The fact that such profound ignorance of basic economics and such self-indulgent emotionalism should be prevalent at elite institutions of higher education is one of the many deep-seated failures of universities on both sides of the Atlantic.

That "Top One Percent"

People who are in the top one percent in income receive far more than one percent of the attention in the media. Even aside from miscellaneous celebrity bimbos, the top one percent attract all sorts of hand-wringing and finger-pointing.

A recent column by Anna Quindlen in *Newsweek* (or is that *Newsweak*?) laments that "the share of the nation's income going to the top 1 percent is at its highest level since 1928."

Who are those top one percent? For those who would like to join them, the question is: How can you do that?

The second question is easy to answer. Virtually anyone who owns a home in San Francisco, no matter how modest that person's income may be, can join the top one percent instantly just by selling their house.

But that's only good for one year, you may say. What if they don't have another house to sell next year?

Well, they won't be in the top one percent again next year, will they? But that's not unusual.

Americans in the top one percent, like Americans in most income brackets, are not there permanently, despite being talked about and written about as if they are an enduring "class"— especially by those who have overdosed on the magic formula of "race, class and gender," which has replaced thought in many intellectual circles.

At the highest income levels, people are especially likely to be transient at that level. Recent data from the Internal Revenue Service show that more than half the people who were in the top one percent in 1996 were no longer there in 2005.

Among the top one-hundredth of one percent, three-quarters of them were no longer there at the end of the decade.

These are not permanent classes but mostly people at current income levels reached by spikes in income that don't last.

These income spikes can occur for all sorts of reasons. In addition to selling homes in inflated housing markets like San Francisco, people can get sudden increases in income from inheritances, or from a gamble that pays off, whether in the stock market, the real estate market, or Las Vegas.

Some people's income in a particular year may be several times what it has ever been before or will ever be again.

Among corporate CEOs, those who cash in stock options that they have accumulated over the years get a big spike in income the year that they cash them in. This lets critics quote inflated incomes of the top-paid CEOs for that year. Some of these incomes are almost as large as those of big-time entertainers— who are never accused of "greed," by the way.

Just as there may be spikes in income in a given year, so there are troughs in income, which can be just as misleading in the hands of those who are ready to grab a statistic and run with it.

Many people who are genuinely affluent, or even rich, can have business losses or an off year in their profession, so that their income in a given year may be very low, or even negative, without their being poor in any meaningful sense.

This may help explain such things as hundreds of thousands of people with incomes below $20,000 a year living in homes that cost $300,000 and up. Many low-income people also have swimming pools or other luxuries that they could not afford if their incomes were permanently at their current level.

There is no reason for people to give up such luxuries because of a bad year, when they have been making a lot more money in previous years and can expect to be making a lot more money in future years.

Most Americans in the top fifth, the bottom fifth, or any of the fifths in between, do not stay there for a whole decade, much less for life. And most certainly do not remain permanently in the top one percent or the top one-hundredth of one percent.

Most income statistics do not follow given individuals from year to year, the way Internal Revenue Service statistics do. But those other statistics can create the misleading illusion that they do by comparing income brackets from year to year, even though people are moving in and out of those brackets all the time.

That especially includes the top one percent, who have become the focus of so much angst and so much rhetoric.

Race and Economics

Andrew Young's statement that blacks have been "ripped off" by stores run by Jews, Koreans, and Arabs has been rightly criticized and he has apologized. But these irresponsible remarks have wider implications than Andrew Young and wider implications than their political repercussions.

For decades, one of the biggest blind spots of most civil rights "leaders" and "spokesmen" for the black community has been their utter lack of knowledge of economics.

As a purely factual matter, prices do tend to be higher— and the quality of service and products lower— in stores in low-income neighborhoods. But the knee-jerk assumption that this represents "exploitation" or "racism" ignores the economics of the situation.

Many of the ghetto stores charging high prices are struggling to survive, while supermarkets in other neighborhoods are very profitable charging lower prices. There are many reasons for this.

The reason least likely to be acknowledged by those who blame the store owners is that crime, shoplifting, vandalism, and riots have raised the costs, both directly and by causing insurance rates and the costs of security to be higher in ghetto neighborhoods.

The costs of delivering goods to small neighborhood stores are also higher than the costs of delivering goods to huge supermarkets. Delivering a hundred cartons of milk to a supermarket is cheaper than delivering ten cartons of milk to each of ten local stores scattered around town.

Selling a customer $50 worth of groceries in a supermarket takes less time than selling ten customers $5 worth of groceries in a little neighborhood store. Faster turnover is one of the keys to a supermarket's lower prices.

A supermarket can prosper with one cent of clear profit on each dollar of sales because that dollar comes back to be re-used again and again in the course of a year.

If the inventory of a supermarket sells out in two weeks, that one cent comes back 26 times in the course of a year. This means that a penny of profit on a dollar from each sale becomes more than a quarter on a dollar annually.

Few local stores can match that. Not only are the delivery and overhead costs of the local store likely to be higher, the slowness with which its inventory turns over means that even higher prices may not fully compensate for such differences.

The cumulative effect of such cost differences is that prices are often higher and at the same time profit rates lower in poor neighborhoods.

One of the factors limiting what a ghetto store can charge is that many ghetto residents already shop in other neighborhoods, when the price savings are enough to cover bus fare or taxi fare.

Every increase in prices risks losing still more customers.

Many of the same black "leaders" who accuse local store owners of making exorbitant profits also complain that supermarkets seldom locate in ghetto neighborhoods. Do they think supermarkets are against making money, if ghettos are so profitable?

The poor quality of many goods and of the service in ghetto stores is also a result of what has happened in these neighborhoods over the years.

My niece, living in the same Harlem neighborhood where I grew up in the 1940s, often complained of rude service and bad quality goods, as well as their high prices— complaints that were not at all what I experienced growing up in that same neighborhood.

There were far more stores back in the 1940s and it would have been financial suicide for any given store to treat its customers the way ghetto stores can get away with treating them today.

What happened in between? Ghetto riots happened, beginning in the 1960s. Many stores that were looted or burned out in those riots never re-opened. Nor were many other people ready to come in from outside to replace them. Nor were local residents.

People who have neither the efficiency nor the courtesy to compete with other stores in middle-class neighborhoods can survive running ghetto stores because of the lack of competition.

Many black "leaders" and "spokesmen" who romanticized ghetto riots as "uprisings" against oppression are now displaying their ignorance of both history and economics. Those ghetto residents who had nothing to do with those riots are still paying the price.

The "Costs" of Medical Care

We are incessantly being told that the cost of medical care is "too high"— either absolutely or as a growing percentage of our incomes. But nothing that is being proposed by the government is likely to lower those costs, and much that is being proposed is almost certain to increase the costs.

There is a fundamental difference between reducing costs and simply shifting costs around, like a pea in a shell game at a carnival. Costs are not reduced simply because you pay less at a doctor's office and more in taxes— or more in insurance premiums, or more in higher prices for other goods and services that you buy, because the government has put the costs on businesses that pass those costs on to you.

Costs are not reduced simply because you don't pay them. It would undoubtedly be cheaper for me to do without the medications that keep me alive and more vigorous in my old age than people of a similar age were in generations past.

Letting old people die would undoubtedly be cheaper than keeping them alive— but that does not mean that the costs have gone down. It just means that we refuse to pay the costs. Instead, we pay the consequences. There is no free lunch.

Providing free lunches to people who go to hospital emergency rooms is one of the reasons for the current high costs of medical care for others. Politicians mandating what insurance companies must cover is another free lunch that leads to higher premiums for medical insurance— and fewer people who can afford it.

Despite all the demonizing of insurance companies, pharmaceutical companies or doctors for what they charge, the fundamental costs of goods and services are the costs of producing them.

If highly paid chief executives of insurance companies or pharmaceutical companies agreed to work free of charge, it would make very little difference in the cost of insurance or medications. If doctors' incomes were cut in half, that would not lower the cost of producing doctors through years of expensive training in medical schools and hospitals, nor the overhead costs of running doctors' offices.

What it would do is reduce the number of very able people who are willing to take on the high costs of a medical education when the return on that investment is greatly reduced and the aggravations of dealing with government bureaucrats are added to the burdens of the work.

Britain has had a government-run medical system for more than half a century and it has to import doctors, including some from Third World countries where the medical training may not be the best. In short, reducing doctors' income is not reducing the cost of medical care, it is refusing to pay those costs. Like other ways of refusing to pay costs, it has consequences.

Any one of us can reduce medical costs by refusing to pay them. In our own lives, we recognize the consequences. But when someone with a gift for rhetoric tells us that the government can reduce the costs without consequences, we are ready to believe in such political miracles.

There are some ways in which the real costs of medical care can be reduced but the people who are leading the charge for a government takeover of medical care are not the least bit interested in actually reducing those costs, as distinguished from shifting the costs around or just refusing to pay them.

The high costs of "defensive medicine"— expensive tests, medications and procedures required to protect doctors and hospitals from ruinous lawsuits, rather than to help the patients— could be reduced by not letting lawyers get away with filing frivolous lawsuits.

If a court of law determines that the claims made in such lawsuits are bogus, then those who filed those claims could be forced to reimburse those who have been sued for all their expenses, including their attorneys' fees and the lost time of people who have other things to do. But politicians who get huge campaign contributions from lawyers are not about to pass laws to do this.

Why should they, when it is so much easier just to start a political stampede with fiery rhetoric and glittering promises?

The "Costs" of Medical Care:
Part II

Although it is cheaper to buy a pint of milk than to buy a quart of milk, nobody considers that to be lowering the price of milk. Although it is cheaper to buy a lower quality of all sorts of goods than to buy a higher quality, nobody thinks of that as lowering the price of either lower or higher quality goods. Yet, when it comes to medical care, there seems to be remarkably little attention paid to questions of both quantity and quality, in the rush to "bring down the cost of medical care."

There is no question that you can reduce the payments for medical care by having either a lower quantity or a lower quality of medical care. That has already been done in countries with government-run medical systems.

In the United States, the government has already reduced payments for patients on Medicare and Medicaid, with the result that some doctors no longer accept new patients with Medicare or Medicaid. That has not reduced the cost of medical care. It has reduced the availability of medical care, just as buying a pint of milk reduces the payment below what a quart of milk would cost.

Letting old people die instead of saving their lives will undoubtedly reduce medical payments considerably. But old people have that option already—and seldom choose to exercise it, despite clever people who talk about a "duty to die."

A government-run system will take that decision out of the hands of the elderly or their families, and thereby "bring down the cost of medical care." A stranger's death is much easier to take, especially if you are a bureaucrat making that decision in Washington.

At one time, in desperately poor societies, living on the edge of starvation, old people might be abandoned to their fate or even go off on their own to face death alone. But, in a society where huge flat-screen TVs are common, along with a thousand gadgets for amusement and entertainment, and where even most people living below the official poverty line own a car or truck, to talk about a "duty to die" so that younger people can live it up is obscene.

You can even save money by cutting down on medications to relieve pain, as is already being done in Britain's government-run medical system. You can save money by not having as many high-tech medical devices like CAT scans or MRIs, and not using the latest medications. Countries with government-run medical systems have less of all these things than the United States has.

But reducing these things is not "bringing down the cost of medical care." It is simply refusing to pay those costs— and taking the consequences.

For those who live by talking points, one of their biggest talking points is that Americans do not get any longer life span than people in other Western nations by all the additional money we spend on medical care.

Like so many clever things that are said, this argument depends on confusing very different things— namely, "health care" and "medical care." Medical care is a limited part of health care. What we do and don't do in the way we live our lives affects our health and our longevity, in many cases more so than what doctors can do to provide medical care.

Americans have higher rates of obesity, homicide and narcotics addiction than people in many other Western nations. There are severe limits on what doctors and medical care can do about that.

If we are serious about medical care— and we should be serious, since it is a matter of life and death— then we should have no time for clever statements that confuse instead of clarifying.

If we want to compare the effects of medical care, as such, in the United States with that in other countries with government-run medical systems, then we need to compare things where medical care is what matters most, such as survival rates of people with cancer.

The United States has one of the highest rates of cancer survival in the world— and for some cancers, the number one rate of survival. We also lead the world in creating new life-saving pharmaceutical drugs. But all of this can change— for the worse— if we listen to clever people who think they should be running our lives.

The "Costs" of Medical Care: Part III

One of the strongest talking points of those who want a government-run medical care system is that we simply cannot afford the high and rising costs of medical care under the current system.

First of all, what we can afford has absolutely nothing to do with the cost of producing anything. We will either pay those costs or not get the benefits. Moreover, if we cannot afford the quantity and quality of medical care that we want now, the government has no miraculous way of enabling us to afford it in the future.

If you think the government can lower medical costs by eliminating "waste, fraud and abuse," as some Washington politicians claim, the logical question is: Why haven't they done that already?

Over the years, scandal after scandal has shown waste, fraud and abuse to be rampant in Medicare and Medicaid. Why would anyone imagine that a new government medical program will do what existing government medical programs have clearly failed to do?

If we cannot afford to pay for doctors, hospitals and pharmaceutical drugs now, how can we afford to pay for doctors, hospitals and pharmaceutical drugs, in addition to a new federal bureaucracy to administer a government-run medical system?

Nothing is easier for politicians than to rail against the profits of pharmaceutical companies, the pay of doctors and other things that have very little to do with the total cost of medical care, but which can arouse emotions to the point where facts don't matter. As former Congressman Dick Armey put it, "Demagoguery beats data" in politics.

Economics and politics confront the same fundamental problem: What everyone wants adds up to more than there is. Market economies deal with this problem by confronting individuals with the costs of producing what they want, and letting those individuals make their own trade-offs when presented with prices that convey those costs. That leads to self-rationing, in the light of each individual's own circumstances and preferences.

Politics deals with the same problem by making promises that cannot be kept, or which can be kept only by creating other problems that cannot be acknowledged when the promises are made.

Price controls are a classic example. At various times and places, in countries around the world, price controls have been put on any number of goods and services—going all the way back to the days of the Roman Empire and ancient Babylon.

Price controls create lower prices for open and legal transactions— but also black markets where the prices are higher than they were before, because the risks of punishment for illegal activity have to be compensated. Price controls also lead to shortages and quality deterioration.

But politicians who take credit for lower prices blame all these bad consequences on others. Diocletian did this in the days of the Roman Empire, leaders of the French Revolution did this when their price controls on food led to hungry and angry people, and American politicians denounced the oil companies when price controls on gasoline led to long lines at filling stations in the 1970s. It is the same story, whatever the country, the times or the product or service.

The self-rationing that people do when prices are free to convey the inherent impossibility of any economy to supply as much as everybody wants is replaced, under price controls, with rationing imposed by government, which cannot possibly have the same knowledge of each individual's circumstances and preferences— least of all when it comes to medical care, where patients differ in innumerable ways.

Here, as elsewhere, there is no free lunch— even though politicians get elected by promising free lunches. A free lunch in medical care is one of the most dangerous illusions of all.

Waiting in long gasoline lines at filling stations was exasperating back in the 1970s, but waiting weeks to get an MRI to find out why you are sick, and then waiting months for an operation, as happens in countries with government-run medical systems, can be not only painful but dangerous.

You can be dead by the time they find out what is wrong with you and do something about it. But that will "bring down the cost of medical care" because you won't be around to require any.

The "Costs" of Medical Care:
Part IV

What is so wrong with the current medical system in the United States that we are being urged to rush headlong into a new government-run system that we are not even supposed to understand, because this legislation is to be rushed through Congress before even the Senators and Representatives have a chance to read it?

Among the things that people complain about under the present medical care system are the costs, insurance company bureaucrats' denials of reimbursements for some treatments and the freeloaders at hospital emergency rooms whose costs have to be paid by others.

Will a government-run medical system make these things better or worse? This very basic question seldom seems to get asked, much less answered.

If the government has some magic way of reducing costs— rather than shifting them around, including shifting them to the next generation— they have certainly not revealed that secret. The actual track record of government when it comes to costs— of anything— is more alarming than reassuring.

What about insurance companies denying reimbursements for treatments? Does anyone imagine that a government bureaucracy will not do that?

Moreover, the worst that an insurance company can do is refuse to pay for medication or treatment. In some countries with government-run medical systems, the government can prevent you from spending your own money to get the medication or treatment that their bureaucracy has denied you. Your choice is to leave the country or smuggle in what you need.

However appalling such a situation may be, it is perfectly consistent with elites wanting to control your life. As far as those elites are concerned, it would not be "social justice" to allow some people to get medical care that others are denied, just because some people "happen to have money."

But very few people just "happen to have money." Most people have earned money by producing something that other people wanted. But getting what you want by what you have earned, rather than by what elites will deign to allow you to have, is completely incompatible with the vision of an elite-controlled world, which they call "social justice" or other politically attractive phrases.

The "uninsured" are another big talking point for government medical insurance. But the incomes of many of the uninsured indicate that many— if not most— of them choose to be uninsured. Poor people can get insurance through Medicaid.

Free-loading at emergency rooms— mandated by government— makes being uninsured a viable option.

Within living memory, most Americans had no medical insurance. Even large medical bills were paid off over a period of months or years, just as we buy big-ticket items like cars or houses.

This is not ideal for everybody or every situation. But if we are ready to rush headlong into government control of our lives every time something is not ideal, then we are not going to remain a free people very long.

Ironically, it is politicians who have already made medical insurance so expensive that many people refuse to buy it. Insurance is designed to cover risk. But politicians have mandated that insurance cover things that are not risks and that neither the buyers nor the sellers of insurance want covered.

In various states, medical insurance must cover the costs of fertility treatments, annual checkups and other things that have nothing to do with risks. What many people most want is to be insured against the risk of having their life's savings wiped out by a catastrophic illness.

But you cannot get insurance just for catastrophic illnesses when politicians keep piling on mandates that drive up the cost of the insurance. These are usually state mandates but the federal government is already promising more mandates on insurance companies— which means still higher costs and higher premiums.

All this makes a farce of the notion of a "public option" that will simply provide competition to keep private insurance companies honest. What politicians can and will do is continue to drive up the cost of private insurance until it is no longer viable. A "public option" is simply a path toward a "single payer" system, a euphemism for a government monopoly.

Jobs or Snow Jobs?

President Obama keeps talking about the jobs his administration is "creating" but there are more people unemployed now than before he took office. How can there be more unemployment after so many jobs have been "created"?

Let's go back to square one. What does it take to create a job? It takes wealth to pay someone who is hired, not to mention additional wealth to buy the material that person will use.

But government creates no wealth. Ignoring that plain and simple fact enables politicians to claim to be able to do all sorts of miraculous things that they cannot do in fact. Without creating wealth, how can they create jobs? By taking wealth from others, whether by taxation, selling bonds or imposing mandates.

However it is done, transferring wealth is not creating wealth. When government uses transferred wealth to hire people, it is essentially transferring jobs from the private sector, not adding to the net number of jobs in the economy.

If that was all that was involved, it would be a simple verbal fraud, with no gain of jobs and no net loss. In reality, many other things that politicians do reduce the number of jobs.

Politicians who mandate various benefits that employers must provide for workers gain politically by seeming to give people something for nothing. But making workers more expensive means that fewer are likely to be hired.

During an economic recovery, employers can respond to an increased demand for their companies' products by hiring more workers— creating more jobs— or they can work their existing employees overtime. Since workers have to be paid time-and-a-half for overtime, it might seem as if it would always be cheaper to hire more workers. But that was before politicians began mandating more benefits per worker.

When you get more hours of work from the existing employees, you don't need to pay for additional mandates, as you would have to when you get more hours of work by hiring new people. For many employers, that makes it cheaper to pay for overtime. The data show that overtime hours have been increasing in the economy while more people have been laid off.

There is another way of reducing the cost of government-imposed mandates. That is by hiring temporary workers, to whom the mandates do not apply.

The number of temporary workers hired has increased for the fourth consecutive month, even though there are millions of unemployed people who could be hired for regular jobs, if it were not for the mandates that politicians have imposed.

Economists have long been saying that there is no free lunch, but politicians get elected by seeming to give free lunches, in one form or another. Yet there are no magic wands in Washington to make costs disappear, whether with workers or with medical care. We just pay in a different way, often a more costly way.

Nor can these costs all be simply dumped on "the rich," because there are just not enough of them. Often people who are far from rich pay the biggest price in lost opportunities. A classic example is the minimum wage law.

Minimum wage laws appear to give low-income workers something for nothing— and appearances are what count in politics. Realities can be left to others, so long as appearances get votes.

People with low skills or little experience usually get paid low wages. Passing a minimum wage law does not make them any more valuable. At a higher wage, it can just make them expendable. Raising the minimum wage in the midst of a recession was guaranteed to increase unemployment among the young— and it has.

None of this is peculiar to the current administration. The Roosevelt administration created huge numbers of government jobs during the 1930s— and yet unemployment remained in double digits throughout FDR's first two terms.

Constant government experiments with new bright ideas is another common feature of Obama's "change" and FDR's New Deal. The uncertainty that this unpredictable experimentation generates makes employers reluctant to hire. Destroying some jobs while creating other jobs does not get you very far, except politically. But politically is what matters to politicians, even if their policies needlessly prolong a recession or depression.

A Glimmer of Hope

It was a common political move when Chicago's city council voted recently to impose a $10 an hour minimum wage on big-box retailers. There is nothing that politicians like better than handing out benefits to be paid for by someone else.

What was uncommon was the reaction. Chicago's Mayor Richard M. Daley denounced the bill as "redlining," since it would have the net effect of keeping much-needed stores and jobs out of black neighborhoods. Both Chicago newspapers also denounced the bill.

The crowning touch came when Andrew Young, former civil rights leader and former mayor of Atlanta, went to Chicago to criticize local black leaders who supported this bill.

While the $10 an hour minimum wage was politics as usual, the unusual backlash against it provides at least a glimmer of hope that more people are beginning to consider the economic consequences of such feel-good legislation.

A survey has shown that 85 percent of the economists in Canada and 90 percent of the economists in the United States say that minimum wage laws reduce employment. But you don't need a Ph.D. in economics to know that jacking up prices leads fewer people to buy. Those people include employers, who hire less labor when labor is made artificially more expensive.

It happens in France, it happens in South Africa, it happens in New Zealand. How surprised should we be when it happens in Chicago?

The economic consequence of political largess— whether in the form of minimum wage laws or medical or other benefits mandated to be paid for by employers— is to make labor artificially more expensive.

Countries with generous employee benefits mandated by law— Germany and France, for example— have chronically higher unemployment rates than unemployment rates in the United States, where jobs are created at a far higher rate than in Europe.

There is no free lunch. Higher labor costs mean fewer jobs.

Since all workers do not have the same skill or experience, minimum wage laws have more impact on some than on others. Young, inexperienced and unskilled workers are especially likely to find it harder to get a job when wage rates have been set higher than the value of their productivity.

In France, where the national unemployment rate is 10 percent, the unemployment rate among workers less than 26 years old is 23 percent. Among young people from the Muslim minority, the unemployment rate is even higher.

In the United States, the group hardest hit by minimum wage laws are black male teenagers. Those who refuse to admit that the minimum wage is the reason for high unemployment rates among young blacks blame racism, lack of education and whatever else occurs to them.

The hard facts say otherwise. Back in the 1940s, there was no less racism than today and black teenagers had no more education than today, but their unemployment rate was a fraction of what it is now—and was no different from that of white teenagers.

What was different back then? Although there was a minimum wage law on the books, the inflation of that era had raised wage rates well above the specified minimum, which had remained unchanged for years.

For all practical purposes, there was no minimum wage law. Only after the minimum wage began to be raised, beginning in 1950, and escalating repeatedly in the years thereafter, did black teenage unemployment skyrocket.

Most studies show unemployment resulting from minimum wages. But a few studies that reach different conclusions are hailed as having "refuted" the "myth" that minimum wages cause unemployment.

Some of these latter studies involve surveying employers before and after a minimum wage increase. But you can only survey employers who are still in business. By surveying people who played Russian roulette and are still around, you could "refute" the "myth" that Russian roulette is dangerous.

Minimum wage laws play Russian roulette with people who need jobs and the work experience that will enable them to rise to higher pay levels. There is now a glimmer of hope that more people are beginning to understand this, despite political demagoguery.

An Off-Budget Office?

Under the headline "Costly Bill Seen as Saving Money," the *San Francisco Chronicle* last week began a front-page story with these words: "Many people find it hard to understand how the health care legislation heading for a decisive vote Sunday can cost $940 billion and cut the horrendous federal deficit at the same time."

It's not hard to understand at all. It is a lie.

What makes this particular lie pass muster with many people, who might otherwise use their common sense, is that the Congressional Budget Office has put their seal of approval on the budget numbers that say you can add millions of people to a government-run system and yet save money.

The Congressional Budget Office does honest work. But it can only use the numbers that Congress supplies— and Congress does dishonest work. It is not the Congressional Budget Office's job to give their opinion as to whether any of the marvelous things that Congress says it will do in the future are either likely or possible.

The Congressional Budget Office is like a computer: Garbage in, garbage out. The numbers in the health care bill are especially smelly garbage.

Do we really need a government agency to give us a false sense of security? Don't we already have politicians to do that? Weren't they doing that at the height of the housing boom that preceded the collapse that brought down the whole financial system and the whole economy? Many warnings were brushed aside.

What we really need— and will never get— is a Congressional Off-Budget Office. This would be an agency that does not have to accept whatever numbers Congress sends them and pretend to take those numbers seriously.

An independent agency could add up all of the government's financial liabilities, whether they are in the official budget or not. For example, the Federal Deposit Insurance Corporation, which guarantees bank accounts, has only a fraction of the money that it is supposed to have on hand to see that people's life savings don't get wiped out when a bank fails.

No administration of either party is going to let people's life savings get wiped out. That would be political suicide. FDIC is definitely too big to fail. But none of the billions of dollars that will be necessary to pour into FDIC at some point, as banks continue to fail and the FDIC's reserves shrink, appears in the official budget numbers that the Congressional Budget Office sees.

It is a similar story with the Federal Housing Administration, which has what the *Wall Street Journal* calls "razor thin reserves" as it goes around the country, merrily guaranteeing ever larger mortgages for ever larger numbers of people, while 14 percent of these mortgages are already delinquent.

When the FHA is finally scraping the bottom of the barrel, trying to come up with the money to redeem all the reckless— but politically popular— guarantees it is making, where do you think that additional money they need will come from? From taxpayers— current and future.

But none of this money is in the official federal budget that the Congressional Budget Office sees. There are many other financial liabilities of the government that are "off-budget," which means that they do not show up in the official numbers.

What if an individual operated this way? If you are 80 years old, and your assets exactly balance your liabilities, you're in good shape, right? Wrong.

At your age, you know that there may be some big medical bills coming, somewhere down the road. If you have been following politics— which may be bad for your blood pressure— you know that the mountainous federal deficits that extend into the future, as far as the eye can see, are likely to set off inflation that will silently steal a big chunk of the value of whatever money you have put aside for your old age. But none of that shows up in the numbers measuring your current assets and liabilities.

Moreover, at 80 years of age, you are not likely to be able to resume a career and make anything like the money you once made. What can you do? Unlike the federal government, you cannot just send your official numbers over to the Congressional Budget Office and have them announce that you are in great financial shape.

CULTURAL ISSUES

Politics, economics and war are all exciting, but culture is often quietly decisive. You cannot explain why France, which fought off the German invaders for four long years during the First World War, despite devastating casualties, collapsed and surrendered after just six weeks of fighting in the Second World War, on the basis of objective factors. Both the German and the French military leaders at the time thought at the outset that France had the better prospects of victory. Decades later, German and French military scholars reached the same conclusion. But the culture of France had changed between the World Wars. Hitler followed such things, and banked on the French no longer being the same when he over-ruled all the protests of his generals and ordered the invasion of France to begin in 1940, when some of those generals thought they were being sent on a suicidal mission.

Race may be visible on the surface but culture goes deep. Americans are not a race but the American culture is what has made Americans different from the various races of Europe, Asia and Africa from which Americans are derived. People of the same race will slaughter each other when they come from different cultures. Generals of German ancestry— Pershing and Eisenhower— led the American armies against Germany in both World Wars, and German cities were bombed into rubble by another American general of German ancestry, Carl Spaatz.

War is not the only arena where culture is decisive. A culture pervaded by corruption will keep a country poor, even if it has an abundance of rich natural resources. Youngsters from a culture that puts a high value on education outperform youngsters from a culture that does not, even when they live at the same economic level, in the same neighborhoods and sit side-by-side in the same schools.

Cultures are inherited, just like race, and may be nearly as hard to change. Cultural head starts have enduring consequences. Because Western Europe was invaded by the Romans, it acquired written languages centuries before Eastern Europe did and remained more advanced for centuries, as literate societies have been more advanced than illiterate societies around the world.

Cultures do change, however, and— like other changes— these may be for better or for worse. Many of the cultural changes in contemporary America, and in Western civilization in general, have been for the worse. These changes are among the many ingredients of a gathering perfect storm.

Taking America for Granted

When my research assistant and her husband took my wife and me to dinner at a Chinese restaurant, I was impressed when I heard her for the first time speak Chinese as she ordered food.

My assistant was born and raised in China, so I should have been impressed that she spoke English. But I took that for granted because she always spoke English to me.

We all have a tendency to take for granted what we are used to, and to regard it as somehow natural or automatic— and to be unduly impressed by what is unusual.

Too many Americans take the United States for granted and are too easily impressed by what people in other countries say and do.

That is especially true of the intelligentsia, and dangerously true of those Supreme Court justices who cite foreign laws when making decisions about American law.

There is nothing automatic about the way of life achieved in this country. It is very unusual among the nations of the world today and rarer than four-leaf clovers in the long view of history.

It didn't just happen. People made it happen— and they and those who came after them paid a price in blood and treasure to create and preserve this nation that we now take for granted.

More important, this country's survival is not automatic. What we do will determine that.

Too many Americans today are not only unconcerned about what it will take to preserve this country but are busy dismantling the things that make it America.

Our national motto, "E Pluribus Unum"— from many, one— has been turned upside down as educators, activists and politicians strive to fragment the American population into separate racial, social, linguistic and ideological blocs.

Some are gung ho for generic "change"— without the slightest concern that the change might be for the worse, even in a world where most nations that are different are also worse off. Most are worse off economically and many are much worse off in terms of despotism, corruption, and bloodshed.

History is full of nations and even whole civilizations that have fallen from the heights to destitution and disintegration.

The Roman Empire is a classic example, but the great ancient Chinese dynasties, the Ottoman Empire and many others have met the same fate.

These were not just political "changes." They were historic catastrophes from which whole peoples did not recover for centuries. It has been estimated that it was a thousand years before Europeans again achieved as high a standard of living as they had in Roman times. The Dark Ages were called dark for a reason.

Today, whole classes of people get their jollies and puff themselves up by denigrating and denouncing American society.

Such people are a major influence in our media, in our educational system and among all sorts of vocal activists.

Nothing illustrates their power to distort reality like the way they seize upon slavery to denounce American society.

Slavery was cancerous but does anybody regard cancer in the United States as an evil peculiar to American society? It is a worldwide affliction and so was slavery.

Both the enslavers and the enslaved have included people on every inhabited continent— people of every race, color, and creed.

More Europeans were enslaved and taken to North Africa by Barbary Coast pirates alone than there were African slaves taken to the United States and to the colonies from which it was formed.

Yet throughout our educational system, our media, and in politics, slavery is incessantly presented as if it were something peculiar to black and white Americans.

What was peculiar about the United States was that it was the first country in which slavery was under attack from the moment the country was created.

What was peculiar about Western civilization was that it was the first civilization to destroy slavery, not only within its own countries but in other countries around the world as well.

Reality has been stood on its head so that a relative handful of people can feel puffed up or gain notoriety and power. Whatever they gain, the rest of us have everything to lose.

De-Programming Students

L etters from parents often complain of a sense of futility in trying to argue with their own children, who have been fed a steady diet of the politically correct vision of the world, from elementary school to the university.

Some ask for suggestions of particular books that might make a dent in the know-it-all attitude of some young people who have heard only one side of the story in classrooms all their lives.

That is one way of going about trying to de-program young people. There are, for example, some good books showing what is wrong with the "global warming" crusades or showing why male-female differences in income or occupations are not automatically discrimination.

Various authors have written a lot of good books that demolish what is currently believed— and taught to students— on a wide range of issues. Some of those books are listed as suggested readings on my website (www.tsowell.com).

Yet trying to undo the propaganda that passes for education at too many schools and colleges, one issue at a time, may not always be the best strategy. There are too many issues on which the politically correct party line is considered to be the only way to look at things.

Cultural Issues

Given the wide range of issues on which students are indoctrinated, instead of being educated, trying to undo all of that would require a whole shelf full of books— and somehow getting the students to read them all.

Another approach might be to respond to the dogmatic certainty of some young person, perhaps your own offspring, by asking: "Have you ever read a single book on the other side of that issue?"

Chances are, after years of being "educated," even at some of the highest-priced schools and colleges, they have not.

When the inevitable answer to your question is "No," you can simply point out how illogical it is to be so certain about anything when you have heard only one side of the story— no matter how often you have heard that one side repeated.

Would it make sense for a jury to reach a verdict after having heard only the prosecution's case, or only the defense attorney's case, but not both?

There is no need to argue the specifics of the particular issue that has come up. You can tell your overconfident young student that you will be happy to discuss that particular issue after he or she has taken the elementary step of reading something by somebody on the other side.

Elementary as it may seem that we should hear both sides of an issue before making up our minds, that is seldom what happens on politically correct issues today in our schools and colleges. The biggest argument of the left is that there is no argument— whether the issue is global warming, "open space" laws or whatever.

Some students may even imagine that they have already heard the other side because their teachers may have given them their version of other people's arguments or motives.

But a jury would never be impressed by having the prosecution tell them what the defendant's defense is. They would want to hear the defense attorney present that case.

Yet most students who have read and heard repeatedly about the catastrophes awaiting us unless we try to stop "global warming" have never read a book, an article or even a single word by any of the hundreds of climate scientists, in countries around the world, who have expressed opposition to that view.

These students may have been shown Al Gore's movie "An Inconvenient Truth" in school, but are very unlikely to have been shown the British Channel 4 television special, "The Great Global Warming Swindle."

Even if we assume, for the sake of argument, that students are being indoctrinated with the correct conclusions on current issues, that would still be irrelevant educationally. Hearing only one side does nothing to equip students with the experience to know how to sort out opposing sides of other issues they will have to confront in the future, after they have left school and need to reach their own conclusions on the issues arising later.

Yet they are the jury that will ultimately decide the fate of this nation.

Attention-Getters

People can get attention either from their accomplishments or from their deliberate attempts to get attention. Today, almost everywhere you look, people seem to be putting their efforts into getting attention.

Wild hairdos, huge tattoos, pierced body parts, outlandish clothing, weird statements— all these have become substitutes for achievements.

Some parents give their children off-the-wall names, as if that is the way to give them some kind of individuality. On the contrary, it means joining a stampede toward showiness.

You don't need a crazy name to become famous. It would be hard to think of plainer names than Jim Brown, Ted Williams, Walter Johnson or Michael Jordan.

It was what they did that made their names famous.

In business, some of the biggest changes in the economy were produced by people with plain names like Henry Ford and Bill Gates. In retailing, some of the biggest names were Richard Sears and Sam Walton.

When you achieve something, you don't need gimmicks. This has been especially apparent in sports.

Joe Louis wore the same standard boxing trunks as everybody else, not the wildly varying and garish trunks that so many boxers wear today.

He did not find it necessary to taunt or denigrate his opponents or behave like a lout inside or outside the ring. But he scored more first-round knockouts in championship fights than any other heavyweight, and will be remembered as long as boxing is remembered.

If Jim Brown had carried on in the end zone after every touchdown he scored, the way so many football players do today, it is hard to see how he could have had the energy left to average more than five yards a carry for his career.

The problem is not just with people who want to get attention by the way they dress, act, talk, or show off in innumerable other ways. The more fundamental problem is that the society around them pays its attention to such superficial and often childish stuff.

The media attention lavished on Anna Nicole Smith and Paris Hilton 24/7, while paying little attention to Iran's movement toward nuclear weapons that can change the course of history irrevocably, is one of the most painful signs of our times.

A lifetime of making major contributions to the health, prosperity, or education of a whole society will not get as much media attention as organizing some loud and strident demonstration, spiced with runaway rhetoric.

In a "non-judgmental" world, what is there to determine who deserves notice, except who can make a big splash?

We not only live longer today, we are more vigorous in our sixties than earlier generations were in their forties. But can you name even one person or one enterprise that conferred this enormous benefit on millions of people?

The average American today has a standard of living that includes things that only the upper crust could have afforded in times past— and some things that even the rich didn't have in past generations, like personal computers.

But are the people who made that possible even mentioned, much less publicized and praised?

There is not an inventor, scientist, medical researcher, or industrialist who is as well known as loudmouths like Rosie O'Donnell or Jesse Jackson.

Any bimbo who exposes her body can get more attention than someone who finds ways to reduce the cost of housing for millions of people. In California, the bimbo can get favorable attention while the developer is condemned.

In short, the problem is not that particular people do particular things to get attention. The problem is that the society at large no longer has standards by which to deny or rebuke attention-seekers who have nothing to contribute to society.

Do not expect sound judgments in a society where being "non-judgmental" is an exalted value. As someone has said, if you don't stand for something, you will fall for anything.

Mind-Changing Books

From time to time, readers ask me what books have made the biggest difference in my life. I am not sure how to answer that question because the books that happened to set me off in a particular direction at a particular time may have no profound or valuable message for others— and can even be books I no longer believe in today.

The first book that got me interested in political issues was *Actions and Passions* by Max Lerner, which I read at age 19. It was a collection of his newspaper columns, none of which I remember today and all of which were vintage liberalism, which even Max Lerner himself apparently had second thoughts about in his later years.

The writings of Karl Marx— especially *The Communist Manifesto*— had the longest lasting effect on me as a young man and led me to become and remain a Marxist throughout my twenties. I wouldn't recommend *The Communist Manifesto* today either, except as an example of a masterpiece of propaganda.

There was no book that changed my mind about being on the political left. Life experience did that— especially the experience of seeing government at work from the inside.

The book that permanently made me a sadder— and, hopefully, wiser— man was Edward Gibbons' *The*

Decline and Fall of the Roman Empire. To follow one of the greatest civilizations of all time as it degenerated and fractured, even before being torn apart by its enemies, was especially painful in view of the parallels to what is happening in America in our own times.

The fall of the Roman Empire was not just a matter of changing rulers or political systems. It was the collapse of a whole civilization— the destruction of an economy, the breakdown of law and order, the disappearance of many educational institutions.

It has been estimated that a thousand years passed before the standard of living in Western Europe rose again to the level it had once had back in Roman times. How long would it take to recover from the collapse of Western civilization today— if we ever recovered?

The kinds of books most readers seem to have in mind when they ask for my recommendations are books that go to the heart of a particular subject, books that open the eyes of the reader in a mind-changing way.

James Q. Wilson's books on crime are like that, shattering the illusions of the intelligentsia about "root causes," "prevention" programs, "rehabilitation," and other trendy nonsense. Professor Wilson's books are a strong dose of hard facts that counter mushy rhetoric.

Peter Bauer's books on economic development demolish many myths about the causes of poverty in the Third World— and about "foreign aid" as a way of relieving that poverty. The last of these books was the best, *Equality, the Third World, and Economic Delusion*.

If you are interested specifically in why Latin American economies have lagged behind for so long, try reading *Underdevelopment Is a State of Mind* by Lawrence Harrison.

Among my own books, those that the most readers have said changed their minds have been *A Conflict of Visions*, *Basic Economics*, and *Black Rednecks and White Liberals*.

A Conflict of Visions is my own favorite among my books. It traces the underlying assumptions behind opposing ideologies that have dominated the Western world over the past two centuries and are still going strong today. *The Vision of the Anointed* is another book of mine that deals with the same subject, but concentrating on the conflicts of our time, and it is written in a more readable style, not as academic as *A Conflict of Visions*.

The most readable of this list of my books is *Basic Economics*, which may also be the most needed, as suggested by its being translated into six foreign languages.

Black Rednecks and White Liberals challenges much that has been said and accepted, not only about blacks but about Jews, Germans, white Southerners and others.

Experience has probably changed more minds than books have. But some books can pull your experiences together and show how they require a very different vision of the world.

The Great Escape

Many of the issues of our times are hard to understand without understanding the vision of the world that they are part of. Whether the particular issue is education, economics or medical care, the preferred explanation tends to be an external explanation— that is, something outside the control of the individuals directly involved.

Education is usually discussed in terms of the money spent on it, the teaching methods used, class sizes or the way the whole system is organized. Students are discussed largely as passive recipients of good or bad education.

But education is not something that can be given to anybody. It is something that students either acquire or fail to acquire. Personal responsibility may be ignored or downplayed in this "non-judgmental" age, but it remains a major factor nevertheless.

After many students go through a dozen years in the public schools, at a total cost of $100,000 or more per student— and emerge semi-literate and with little understanding of the society in which they live, much less the larger world and its history— most discussions of what is wrong leave out the fact that many such students may have chosen to use school as a place to fool around, act up, organize gangs or even peddle drugs.

The great escape of our times is escape from personal responsibility for the consequences of one's own behavior. Differences in infant mortality rates provoke pious editorials on a need for more prenatal care to be provided by the government for those unable to afford it. In other words, the explanation is automatically assumed to be external to the mothers involved and the solution is assumed to be something that "we" can do for "them."

While it is true that black mothers get less prenatal care than white mothers and have higher infant mortality rates, it is also true that women of Mexican ancestry also get less prenatal care than white women and yet have lower infant mortality rates.

But, once people with the prevailing social vision see the first set of facts, they seldom look for any other facts that might go against the explanation that fits their vision of the world.

No small part of the current confusion between "health care" and medical care comes from failing to recognize that Americans can have the best medical care in the world without having the best health because so many people choose to live in ways that shorten their lives.

There can be grave practical consequences of a dogmatic insistence on external explanations that allow individuals to escape personal responsibility. Americans can end up ruining the best medical care in the world in the vain hope that a government takeover will give us better health.

Economic issues are approached in the same way. People with low incomes are seen as a problem for other people to solve. Studies which follow the same individuals over time show that the vast majority of working people who are in the bottom 20 percent of income earners at a given time end up rising out of that bracket.

Many are simply beginners who get beginners' wages but whose pay rises as they acquire more skills and experience. Yet there is a small minority of workers who do not rise and a large number of people who seldom work and who— surprise!— have low incomes as a result.

Seldom is there any thought that people who choose to waste years of their own time (and the taxpayers' money) in school need to change their own behavior— or to visibly suffer the consequences, so that their fate can be a warning to others coming after them, not to make the same mistake.

It is not just the "non-judgmental" ideology of the intelligentsia but also the self-interest of politicians that leads to so much downplaying of personal responsibility in favor of external explanations and external programs to "solve" the "problem."

On these and other issues, government programs are far less likely to solve the country's problems than to solve the politicians' problem of getting the votes of those who think the answer to every problem is for the government to "do something."

The Fallacy of "Fairness"

I f there is ever a contest to pick which word has done the most damage to people's thinking, and to actions to carry out that thinking, my nomination would be the word "fair." It is a word thrown around by far more people than have ever bothered to even try to define it.

This mushy vagueness may be a big handicap in logic but it is a big advantage in politics. All sorts of people, with very different notions about what is or is not fair, can be mobilized behind this nice-sounding word, in utter disregard of the fact that they mean very different things when they use that word.

Some years ago, for example, there was a big outcry that various mental tests used for college admissions or for employment were biased and "unfair" to many individuals or groups. Fortunately there was one voice of sanity— David Riesman, I believe— who said: "The tests are not unfair. *Life* is unfair and the tests measure the results."

If by "fair" you mean everyone having the same odds for achieving success, then life has never been anywhere close to being fair, anywhere or at any time. If you stop and think about it (however old-fashioned that may seem), it is hard even to conceive of how life could possibly be fair in that sense.

Even within the same family, among children born to the same parents and raised under the same roof, the first-borns on average have higher IQs than their brothers and sisters, and usually achieve more in life.

Unfairness is often blamed on somebody, even if only on "society." But whose fault is it if you were not the first born? Since some groups have more children than others, a higher percentage of the next generation will be first-borns in groups that have smaller families, so such groups have an advantage over other groups.

Despite all the sound and fury generated in controversies over whether different groups have different genetic potential, even if they all have identical genetic potential the outcomes can still differ if they have different birth rates.

Twins have average IQs several points lower than children born singly. Whether that is due to having to share resources in the womb or having to share parents' attention after birth, the fact is what it is— and it certainly is not fair.

Many people fail to see the fundamental difference between saying that a particular thing— whether a mental test or an institution— is conveying a difference that already exists or is creating a difference that would not exist otherwise.

Creating a difference that would not exist otherwise is discrimination, and something can be done about that. But, in recent times, virtually any disparity in outcomes is almost automatically blamed on discrimination, despite the incredible range of other reasons for disparities between individuals and groups.

Nature's discrimination completely dwarfs man's discrimination. Geography alone makes equal chances virtually impossible. The geographic advantages of

Western Europe over Eastern Europe— in climate and navigable waterways, among other things— have led to centuries of differences in income levels that were greater than income differences between blacks and whites in America today.

Just the fact that the lay of the land is different in different parts of Europe meant that it was easier for the Roman legions to invade Western Europe. This meant that Western Europeans had the advantages of the most advanced civilization in Europe at that time. Moreover, because Roman letters were used in Western Europe, the languages of that region had written versions centuries before the Slavic languages of Eastern Europe did.

The difference between literacy and illiteracy is a huge difference, and it remained huge for centuries. Was it the Slavs' fault that the Romans did not want to climb over so many mountains to get to them?

To those living in Western Europe in the days of the Roman Empire, the idea of being conquered, and many slaughtered, by the Romans probably had no great appeal. But their descendants would benefit from their bad luck. And that doesn't seem fair either.

The Fallacy of "Fairness": Part II

A recent flap in a Berkeley high school reveals what a farce "fairness" can be. Because this is ultra-liberal Berkeley, perhaps we should not be surprised that a proposal has been made to eliminate four jobs as science teachers and use the money saved for programs to help low achievers.

In Berkeley, as in many other communities across the country, black and Latino students are not performing as well as Asian and white students. In fact, the racial gap in academic achievement at Berkeley High School is the highest in California— no doubt a special source of embarrassment in politically correct Berkeley. According to the principal, "Our community at Berkeley High School has failed the African-Americans." Therefore "We need to bring everybody up— that's what this plan is about."

Surely no one, not even in Berkeley, seriously believes that you will "bring everybody up" by eliminating science teachers. This is a proposal to redistribute money from science to social work, by providing every student with advisors on note-taking, time management and other learning skills.

The point is to close educational gaps among groups, or at least go on record as trying. As with most equalization crusades, whether in education or in the economy, it is about equalizing downward, by lowering those at the top. "Fairness" strikes again!

This is not just a crazy idea by one principal in Berkeley. It is a crazy idea taught in schools of education across the country. A professor of education at the University of San Francisco has weighed in on the controversy at Berkeley, supporting the idea of "projects designed to narrow the achievement gap."

In keeping with the rhetoric of the prevailing ideology, our education professor refers to "privileged" parents and "privileged" children who want to "forestall any progress toward equity."

In the language of the politically correct, achievement is equated with privilege. Such verbal sleight of hand evades the question whether individuals' own priorities and efforts affect outcomes, whether in education or in other endeavors. No need to look at empirical evidence when a clever phrase can take that whole question off the table.

This verbal sleight of hand is not confined to education. A study of incomes of various groups in Toronto concluded that Canadians of Japanese ancestry were the most "privileged" group in that city. That is, people of Japanese ancestry there had higher incomes than members of other minorities and higher than that of the white majority in Toronto.

What makes the "privileged" label a particularly bad joke in this case is a history of blatant discrimination against the Japanese in Canada in years past, including a longer internment during World War II than that of Japanese Americans. But, to some on the left, the very concept of achievement must be banished by all means necessary, regardless of the facts.

Achievement by overcoming obstacles is a special threat to the left's vision of the world, and so must be magically transformed into privilege through rhetoric.

Those with that vision do not want to even discuss evidence that students from different groups spend different amounts of time on homework and different amounts of time on social activities. To admit that inputs affect outputs, whether in education, in the economy or in other areas, would be to undermine the vision and agenda of the left, and deprive those who believe in that vision of a moral melodrama, starring themselves as defenders of the oppressed and crusaders against the forces of evil.

Redistribution of material resources has a very poor track record when it comes to actually helping those who are lagging, whether in education, in the economy or elsewhere. What they need are the attitudes, priorities and behavior which produce the outcomes desired.

But changing anyone's attitudes, priorities and behavior is a lot harder than taking a stance as defenders of the oppressed and crusaders against the forces of evil.

To the extent that doing the latter misdiagnoses the problem, it makes solving the problem even harder. That does no good for those who are lagging, however much it exalts those who pose as their defenders. "Fairness" indeed!

The Fallacy of "Fairness": Part III

Most of us want to be fair, in the sense of treating everyone equally. We want laws to be applied the same to everyone. We want educational, economic or other criteria for rewards to be the same as well. But this concept of fairness is not only different from prevailing ideas of fairness among many of the intelligentsia, it contradicts their idea of fairness.

People like philosopher John Rawls call treating everyone alike merely "formal" fairness. Professor Rawls advocated "a conception of justice that nullifies the accidents of natural endowment and the contingencies of social circumstances." He called for a society which "arranges" end-results, rather than simply treating everyone the same and letting the chips fall where they may.

This more hands-on concept of fairness gives third parties a much bigger role to play. But whether any human being has ever had the omniscience to determine and undo the many differences among people born into different families and cultures— with different priorities, attitudes and behavior— is a very big question. And to concentrate the vast amount of power needed to carry out that sweeping agenda is a dangerous gamble, whose actual consequences have too often been written on the pages of history in blood.

There is no question that the accident of birth is a huge factor in the fate of people. What is a very serious question is how much anyone can do about that without creating other, and often worse, problems. Providing free public education, scholarships to colleges and other opportunities for achievement are fine as far as they go, but there should be no illusion that they can undo all the differences in priorities, attitudes and efforts among different individuals and groups.

Trying to change whole cultures and subcultures in which different individuals are raised would be a staggering task. But the ideology of multiculturalism, which pronounces all cultures to be equally valid, puts that task off limits. This paints people into whatever corner the accident of birth has put them.

Under these severe constraints, all that is left is to blame others when the outcomes are different for different individuals and groups. Apparently those who are lagging are to continue to think and act as they have in the past— and yet somehow have better outcomes in the future. And, if they don't get the same outcomes as others, then according to this way of seeing the world, it is society's fault!

Society may lavish thousands of dollars per year on schooling for a youngster who does not bother to study, and yet when he or she emerges as a semi-literate adult, it is considered to be society's fault if such youngsters cannot get the same kinds of jobs and incomes as other youngsters who studied conscientiously during their years in school.

It is certainly a great misfortune to be born into families or communities whose values make educational or economic success less likely. But to have intellectuals and others come along and misstate the problem does not help to produce better results, even if it produces a better image.

Political correctness may make it hard for anyone to challenge the image of helpless victims of an evil society. But those who are lagging do not need a better public relations image. They need the ability to produce better results for themselves— and a romantic image is an obstacle to directing their efforts toward developing that ability.

Tests and other criteria which convey the realities of their existing capabilities, compared to that of others, can have what is called a "disparate impact," and are condemned not only in editorial offices but also in courts of law.

But criteria exist precisely to have a disparate impact on those who do not have what these criteria exist to measure. Track meets discriminate against those who are slow afoot. Tests in school discriminate against students who did not study.

Disregarding criteria in the interest of "fairness"— in the sense of outcomes independent of inputs— adds to the handicaps of those who already have other handicaps, by lying to them about the reasons for their situation and the things they need to do to make their situation better.

The Fallacy of "Fairness":
Part IV

Mixed up with the question of fairness to individuals and groups has been the explosive question of whether individuals and groups have the innate ability to perform at the same levels, if they are all treated alike or even given the same objective opportunities.

Intellectuals have swung from one side of this question at the beginning of the 20th century to the opposite side at the end. Both those who said that achievement differences among races and classes were due to genes, in the early years of the 20th century, and those who said that these differences were due to discrimination, in the later years, ignored the old statisticians' warnings that correlation is not causation.

The idea that some people are innately superior (usually one's own group) goes back for centuries, but various new facts that came out in the 19th and early 20th centuries gave the appearance of "science" to such beliefs during the Progressive era.

Sir Francis Galton's research turned up the fact of remarkable achievements among members of the same family, which he regarded as evidence of genetic superiority. The rise of IQ testing, and especially the massive mental testing of soldiers in the U.S. Army during the First World War, showed great differences in test scores among various racial and ethnic groups.

In the public schools, there were similarly large differences in which ethnic group's children failed to get promoted. In both the Army mental tests and in the schools, Polish Jews did poorly at that time. Carl Brigham— a leading authority on mental tests and the author of the SAT— said that the Army tests tended to "disprove the popular belief that the Jew is highly intelligent."

It should be noted that all of these conclusions were based on hard data, not mere "perceptions" or "stereotypes," as so many inconvenient facts are dismissed today. What was wrong were not the data but the inferences.

Polish Jews were among the many immigrants from Eastern Europe and Southern Europe who were relatively recent arrivals in the United States. Many of these immigrants grew up in homes where English was not spoken, as Carl Brigham acknowledged in later years, when he recanted his earlier statements. In later years, Jews scored above average on mental tests.

It is also a hard fact of history that some races had far more advanced technological, economic and other achievements than others at particular times and places. But those who were ahead in some centuries were often behind in other centuries— the Chinese and the Europeans having changed positions dramatically after Europe eventually caught up with China and then surpassed it within recent centuries. But there was no evidence of any dramatic changes in genes among either the Chinese or the Europeans.

Cultural Issues

While striking changes in the relative positions of different races at different periods of history undermine genetic explanations, the fact that there has been no period when their achievements have been the same undermines today's presumption that different economic or other outcomes are due to discrimination.

Whatever the innate capacity of any race, class or other group, what pays off in the real world are developed capabilities, and these have never been the same— or even close to being the same— for individuals or groups.

All the leading brands of beer in the United States were created by people of German ancestry and so was the leading beer in China, not to mention breweries created by Germans in Australia, Argentina and elsewhere. Germans were producing beer in the days of the Roman Empire.

This does not mean that beer brewing skill is genetic but it also does not mean that this skill— or any other skill— is randomly distributed among peoples, so that a failure to have equal "representation" of groups in a given institution can be presumed to be due to discrimination by that institution.

Fairness as equal treatment does not produce fairness as equal outcomes. The confusion between the two meanings of the same word has created enormous mischief, much of it at the expense of lagging groups, who have been distracted from the things that would enable them to catch up. And whole societies have been kept in a turmoil pursuing a will o' the wisp in the name of "fairness."

Adolescent Intellectuals

To a small child, the reason he cannot do many things that he would like to do is that his parents won't let him. Many years later, maturity brings an understanding that there are underlying reasons for doing or not doing many things, and that his parents were essentially conduits for those reasons.

The truly dangerous period in life is the time when the child has learned the limits of his parents' control, and how to circumvent their control, but has not yet understood or accepted the underlying reasons for doing and not doing things. This adolescent period is one that some people— intellectuals especially— never outgrow.

The widespread and fervent use of the word "liberation" in a wide variety of contexts is one of the signs of the adolescent belief that only arbitrary rules and conventions stand in the way of doing whatever we want to do.

According to this vision of the world, the problems of all sorts of individuals and groups— women, minorities, homosexuals, children— are to be solved by liberating them from the restraints of laws, rules, conventions and standards.

They are to be liberated even from the threat of adverse judgments by other individuals. We are all to be "non-judgmental."

Cultural Issues

Two centuries ago, the great British legal scholar William Blackstone pointed out that there are some laws so old that no one remembers why they existed or what purpose they served then or now. But the bad consequences of repealing some of these laws have often made painfully clear what purpose they served.

Some of the painful consequences of various "liberations" that began in the 1960s have included the disintegration of families, skyrocketing crime rates, falling test scores in school, and record-breaking rates of teenage suicide.

A long downward trend in teenage pregnancy and venereal diseases sharply reversed during the 1960s, starting a new trend of escalating teenage pregnancy and venereal diseases, climaxed later by the AIDS epidemic.

Sometimes bad things happen because of adverse circumstances— poverty or war, for example. But our post-1960s social disasters occurred during a long period of peace and unprecedented prosperity. Murder rates, for example, were much lower during the Great Depression of the 1930s and during World War II than they became after various "liberating" changes in the 1960s.

One of the signs of maturity is the ability to learn from experience. Some of us have learned and we have halted or reversed some of the adverse trends. For example, the quest for those elusive "root causes" of crime, so dear to the political left, has been put aside in favor of locking up more criminals— and the crime rate has declined.

The left is upset that we have so many people behind bars and lament how much it is costing to keep them there. They do not even bother to estimate how much it would cost to turn them loose.

The left has never understood why property rights are a big deal, except to fat cats who own a lot of property. Through legislation and judicial rulings, property rights have been eroded with rent control laws, expansive concepts of eminent domain, and all sorts of environmental restrictions.

Some of the biggest losers have been people of very modest incomes and some of the biggest winners have been fat cats who are able to use political muscle and activist judges to violate other people's property rights.

Politicians in cities around the country violate property rights regularly by seizing homes in working-class neighborhoods and demolishing whole sectors of the city, in order to turn the land over to people who will build shopping malls, gambling casinos, and other things that will pay more taxes than the homeowners are paying.

That's why property rights were put in the Constitution in the first place, to keep politicians from doing things like that. But the adolescent intellectuals of our time have promoted the notion that property rights are just arbitrary rules to protect the rich.

Many academics and federal judges are sufficiently insulated from reality by tenure that they never have to grow up.

Ivan and Boris Again

There is an old Russian fable, with different versions in other countries, about two poor peasants, Ivan and Boris. The only difference between them was that Boris had a goat and Ivan didn't. One day, Ivan came upon a strange-looking lamp and, when he rubbed it, a genie appeared. She told him that she could grant him just one wish, but it could be anything in the world.

Ivan said, "I want Boris' goat to die."

Variations on this story in other countries suggest that this tells us something about human beings, not just Russians.

It may tell us something painful about many Americans today, when so many people are preoccupied with the pay of corporate CEOs. It is not that the corporate CEOs' pay affects them so much. If every oil company executive in America agreed to work for nothing, that would not be enough to lower the price of a gallon of gasoline by a dime. If every General Motors executive agreed to work for nothing, that would not lower the price of a Cadillac or a Chevrolet by one percent.

Too many people are like Ivan, who wanted Boris' goat to die.

It is not even that the average corporate CEO makes as much money as any number of professional athletes and entertainers. The average pay of a CEO of a corporation big enough to be included in the Standard & Poor's index is less than one-third of what Alex Rodriguez makes, about one-tenth of what Tiger Woods makes and less than one-thirtieth of what Oprah Winfrey makes.

But when has anyone ever accused athletes or entertainers of "greed"?

It is not the general public that singles out corporate CEOs for so much attention. Politicians and the media have focused on business leaders, and the public has been led along, like sheep.

The logic is simple: Demonize those whose place or power you plan to usurp.

Politicians who want the power to micro-manage business and the economy know that demonizing those who currently run businesses is the opening salvo in the battle to take over their roles.

There is no way that politicians can take over the roles of Alex Rodriguez, Tiger Woods or Oprah Winfrey. So they can make any amount of money they want and it doesn't matter politically.

Those who want more power have known for centuries that giving the people somebody to hate and fear is the key.

In 18th century France, promoting hatred of the aristocracy was the key to Robespierre's acquiring more dictatorial power than the aristocracy had ever had, and using that power to create a bigger bloodbath than anything under the old regime.

In the 20th century, it was both the czars and the capitalists in Russia who were made the targets of public hatred by the Communists on their road to power. That power created more havoc in the lives of more people than czars and capitalists ever had combined.

As in other countries and other times, today it is not just a question of which elites win out in a tug of war in America. It is the people at large who have the most at stake.

We have just seen one of the biggest free home demonstrations of what happens in an economy when politicians tell businesses what decisions to make.

For years, using the powers of the Community Reinvestment Act and other regulatory powers, along with threats of legal action if the loan approval rates varied from the population profile, politicians have pressured banks and other lending institutions into lending to people they would not lend to otherwise.

Yet, when all this blows up in our faces and the economy turns down, what is the answer? To have more economic decisions made by politicians, because they choose to say that "deregulation" is the cause of our problems.

Regardless of how much suffocating regulation may have been responsible for an economic debacle, politicians have learned that they can get away with it if they call it "deregulation."

No matter what happens, for politicians it is "heads I win and tails you lose." If we keep listening to the politicians and their media allies, we are all going to keep losing, big time. Keeping our attention focused on CEO pay— Boris' goat— is all part of this game. We are all goats if we fall for it.

An Investment in Failure

It is not just in Iraq that the political left has an investment in failure. Domestically as well as internationally, the left has long had a vested interest in poverty and social malaise.

The old advertising slogan, "Progress is our most important product," has never applied to the left. Whether it is successful black schools in the United States or Third World countries where millions of people have been rising out of poverty in recent years, the left has shown little interest.

Progress in general seems to hold little interest for people who call themselves "progressives." What arouses them are denunciations of social failures and accusations of wrong-doing.

One wonders what they would do in heaven.

We are in no danger of producing heaven on earth but there have been some remarkable developments in some Third World countries within the past generation that have allowed many very poor people to rise to a standard of living that was never within their reach before.

The August 18, 2007 issue of the distinguished British magazine *The Economist* reveals the economic progress in Brazil, Argentina, and other Latin American nations that has given a better life to millions of their poorest citizens.

Cultural Issues

Some of the economic policies that have led to these results are discussed in *The Economist* but it is doubtful that members of the political left will stampede there to find out what those policies were.

They have shown no such interest in how tens of millions of people in China and tens of millions of people in India have risen out of poverty within the past generation.

Despite whatever the left may say, or even believe, about their concern for the poor, their actual behavior shows their interest in the poor to be greatest when the poor can be used as a focus of the left's denunciations of society.

When the poor stop being poor, they lose the attention of the left. What actions on the part of the poor, or what changes in the economy, have led to drastic reductions in poverty seldom arouse much curiosity, much less celebration.

This is not a new development in our times. Back in the 19th century, when Karl Marx presented his vision of the impoverished working class rising to attack and destroy capitalism, he was disappointed when the workers grew less revolutionary over time, as their standards of living improved.

At one point, Marx wrote to his disciples: "The working class is revolutionary or it is nothing."

Think about that. Millions of human beings mattered to him only in so far as they could serve as cannon fodder in his jihad against the existing society.

If they refused to be pawns in his ideological game, then they were "nothing."

No one on the left would say such things so plainly today, even to themselves. But their actions speak louder than words.

Blacks are to the left today what the working class was to Marx in the 19th century— pawns in an ideological game.

Blacks who rise out of poverty are of no great interest to the left, unless the way they do so is by attacking society.

The poverty rate among black married couples has been in single digits since 1994 but the left has shown no more interest in why that is so than they have shown in why many millions of people have risen out of poverty in Latin America or in China and India.

Where progress can be plausibly claimed to be a result of policies favored by the left, then such claims are made.

A whole mythology has grown up that the advancement of minorities and women in America is a result of policies promoted by the left in the 1960s. Such claims are often based on nothing more substantial than ignoring the history of the progress made prior to 1960.

Retrogressions in the wake of the policies of the 1960s are studiously ignored— the runaway crime rates, the disintegration of black families, and the ghetto riots of the 1960s that have left many black communities still barren more than 40 years later.

Whatever does not advance the left agenda is "nothing."

The Underdogs

It is a good reflection on Americans that they tend to be on the side of the underdog. But it is often hard to tell who is in fact the underdog, or why.

Many years ago, there was a big, lumbering catcher named Ernie Lombardi whose slowness afoot was legendary. Someone once said that not only was Ernie Lombardi the slowest man who ever played major league baseball, whoever was second slowest was probably a lot faster runner than Ernie Lombardi.

When Ernie Lombardi came to bat, infielders played back on the outfield grass. That gave them more range in getting to balls that Lombardi hit. They could snare line-drives that would otherwise be base hits. With ground balls, they could easily throw to first base from the outfield grass and get the slow-moving Lombardi out.

Despite all that, Ernie Lombardi had a lifetime batting average of .306 and even led the league in batting a couple of years. But many people said that, if Lombardi had had just average speed, he could have been a .400 hitter.

One day, as a teenager sitting in the Polo Grounds, the stadium where the then New York Giants played, I was privileged to watch a historic event. Ernie Lombardi laid down a bunt!

The crowd went wild. The play took forever, with Lombardi laboriously clumping down to first base—

running as hard as he could, but still not very fast—while the third baseman made a long run in from left field to get to the bunt.

We cheered ourselves hoarse rooting for big Ernie as he doggedly but slowly made his way down the first base line. He barely beat the throw, which set off another explosion of cheers.

We were not just cheering for a home-town player. We were rooting for Lombardi to get revenge on those who had taken advantage of him for so long. We were cheering for the underdog.

But was Lombardi really an underdog? How many players end up their careers with a lifetime batting average over .300 or with two batting titles? Like most of us, Lombardi was handicapped in some ways and privileged in others.

Many people would consider it a handicap to be a black orphan, born in the Jim Crow South during the Great Depression of the 1930s. But the home into which I was adopted had four adults and I was the only child. Many years later, when I was a parent and asked one of the surviving members of that family how old I was when I started walking, she said: "Oh, Tommy, nobody knows when you could walk. Somebody was always carrying you."

You can't buy that. A leading historian of education has said that the New York City public schools were the best in the country during the 1940s. That was when I went to school there. You can't buy that either. Today the classes are smaller, the buildings more modern—but the education itself is a disaster. I got the kind of education that people have to go to expensive private schools to get today.

Perhaps more important, nobody told me that I couldn't make it because I was poor and black, or that I ought to hate white people today because of what some other white people did to my ancestors in some other time.

Nobody sugar-coated the facts of racial discrimination. But Professor Sterling Brown of Howard University, who wrote with eloquent bitterness about racism, nevertheless said to me when I prepared to transfer to Harvard: "Don't come back here and tell me you didn't make it 'cause white folks were mean."

He burned my bridges behind me, the way they used to do with armies going into battle, so that they had no place to retreat to, and so had to fight to win.

One of the problems with trying to help underdogs, especially with government programs, is that they and everyone else start to think of them as underdogs, focusing on their problems rather than their opportunities. Thinking of themselves as underdogs can also dissipate their energies in resentments of others, rather than spending that energy making the most of their own possibilities.

It must have been discouraging for Ernie Lombardi, especially in his early years, to be repeatedly thrown out at first base on balls that would have been base hits for anybody else. But he couldn't let himself dwell on that— not and win two batting titles.

Artificial Stupidity

A woman with a petition went among the crowds attending a state fair, asking people to sign her petition demanding the banning of dihydrogen monoxide. She said it was in our lakes and streams, and now it was in our sweat and urine and tears.

She collected hundreds of signatures to ban dihydrogen monoxide— a fancy chemical name for water. A couple of comedians were behind this ploy. But there is nothing funny about its implications. It is one of the grim and dangerous signs of our times.

This little episode revealed how conditioned we have become, responding like Pavlov's dog when we hear a certain sound— in this case, the sound of some politically correct crusade.

People are all born ignorant but they are not born stupid. Much of the stupidity we see today is induced by our educational system, from the elementary schools to the universities. In a high-tech age that has seen the creation of artificial intelligence by computers, we are also seeing the creation of artificial stupidity by people who call themselves educators.

Educational institutions created to pass on to the next generation the knowledge, experience and culture of the generations that went before them have instead been turned into indoctrination centers to promote whatever notions, fashions or ideologies happen to be in vogue among today's intelligentsia.

Many conservatives have protested against the specifics of the things with which students are being indoctrinated. But that is not where the most lasting harm is done. Many, if not most, of the leading conservatives of our times were on the left in their youth. These have included Milton Friedman, Ronald Reagan and the whole neoconservative movement.

The experiences of life can help people outgrow whatever they were indoctrinated with. What may persist, however, is the lazy habit of hearing one side of an issue and being galvanized into action without hearing the other side— and, more fundamentally, not having developed any mental skills that would enable you to systematically test one set of beliefs against another.

It was once the proud declaration of many educators that "We are here to teach you how to think, not what to think." But far too many of our teachers and professors today are teaching their students what to think, about everything from global warming to the new trinity of "race, class and gender."

Even if all the conclusions with which they indoctrinate their students were 100 percent correct, that would still not be equipping students with the mental skills to weigh opposing views for themselves, in order to be prepared for new and unforeseeable issues that will arise over their lifetimes, after they leave the schools and colleges.

Many of today's "educators" not only supply students with conclusions, they promote the idea that students should spring into action because of these prepackaged conclusions— in other words, vent their feelings and go galloping off on crusades, without either a knowledge of what is said by those on the other side or the intellectual discipline to know how to analyze opposing arguments.

When we see children in elementary schools out carrying signs in demonstrations, we are seeing the kind of mindless groupthink that causes adults to sign petitions they don't understand or— worse yet— follow leaders they don't understand, whether to the White House, the Kremlin or Jonestown.

A philosopher once said that the most important knowledge is knowledge of one's own ignorance. That is the knowledge that too many of our schools and colleges are failing to teach our young people.

It takes a certain amount of knowledge just to understand the extent of one's own ignorance. But our "educators" have given assignments to children not yet a decade old to write letters to members of Congress, or to Presidents, spouting off on issues ranging from nuclear weapons to medical care.

Will Rogers once said that it was not ignorance that was so bad but "all the things we know that ain't so." But our classroom indoctrinators are getting students to think that they know after hearing only one side of an issue. It is artificial stupidity.

Too Many Apologies

Tiger Woods doesn't owe me an apology. Nothing that he has ever done has cost me a dime nor an hour of sleep.

This is not a plea to be "non-judgmental." I am very judgmental about all sorts of things, including Tiger Woods' bad behavior. But that is very different from saying that he somehow owes me an apology.

For all I know, my neighbors may be judgmental when I drive out of my driveway in a 15-year-old car. But they have never said anything to me about it, and I have never offered them an apology. This is not equating driving a 15-year-old car with what Tiger Woods did. But the point is that any apology he might make should be made to his family, who were hurt, not to the public, who might be disappointed in him, but not really hurt.

Public apologies to people who are not owed any apology have become one of the many signs of the mushy thinking of our times. So are apologies for things that somebody else did.

Among the most absurd apologies have been apologies for slavery by politicians. For one thing, slavery is not something you can apologize for, any more than you can apologize for murder.

If someone says to you that he murdered someone near and dear to you, what are you supposed to say? "No problem, we all make mistakes"? Not bloody likely!

Slavery is too serious for an apology and somebody else being a slaveowner is not something for you to apologize for. When somebody who has never owned a slave apologizes for slavery to somebody who has never been a slave, then what began as mushy thinking has degenerated into theatrical absurdity— or, worse yet, politics.

Slavery has existed all over the planet for thousands of years, with black, white, yellow and other races being both slaves and enslavers. Does that mean that everybody ought to apologize to everybody else for what their ancestors did? Or are the only people who are supposed to feel guilty the ones who have money that others want to talk them out of?

This craze for aimless apologies is part of a general loss of a sense of personal responsibility in our time. We are supposed to feel guilty for what other people did but there are a thousand cop-outs for what we ourselves did to those we did it to.

Back in the 1960s, when so many foolish ideas flourished simply because they were new, a *New York Times* columnist tried to make the case that we were all somehow responsible for the assassination of President Kennedy.

That was considered to be Deep Stuff. It made you one of the special folks when you believed that, instead of one of the rest of us poor dumb slobs who believed that the man who shot him was responsible.

Cultural Issues

For more than a century, the intelligentsia have been trying to get us to focus on the "root causes" of crime—supposedly created by "society"— instead of locking up thieves or executing murderers.

If some people don't have the money or the achievements of others, that too is society's fault, in the eyes of those for whom personal responsibility is an outmoded idea.

Personal responsibility is a real problem for those who want to collectivize society and take away our power to make our own decisions, transferring that power to third parties like themselves, who imagine themselves so much wiser and nobler than the rest of us.

Aimless apologies are just one of the incidental symptoms of an increasing loss of a sense of personal responsibility— without which a whole society is in jeopardy.

The police cannot possibly maintain law and order by themselves. Millions of people can monitor their own behavior better than any third parties can. Cops can cope with that segment of society who have no sense of personal responsibility, but not if that segment becomes a large part of the whole population.

Yet increasing numbers of educators and the intelligentsia seem to have devoted themselves to undermining or destroying a sense of personal responsibility and making "society" responsible instead. Aimless apologies are just one small symptom of this larger and more dangerous attitude.

The Bullet Counters

"Killing an Unarmed Man." That is how the front-page headline in the *New York Times* characterized an incident in which a man tried to run over a policeman with his car and was shot by three policemen on the scene, including his intended victim.

An automobile is a deadly weapon. If you are killed by an automobile, you are just as dead as if you had been shot through the heart.

A phrase like "an unarmed man" makes a talking point— as if matters of life and death should be discussed in terms of how you can spin a talking point.

The biggest and most common talking point when the police fire at someone is counting how many bullets they fired. There are politicians, media people and— above all— community activists who can work themselves into a rage over how many bullets were fired.

If we stop and think— which of course the demagogues hope we will never do— it is hard to see any moral difference between killing someone with one bullet or with dozens of bullets.

People who have never fired a gun in their lives say that they cannot understand why the police fired so many bullets. If it is something that they have never experienced, there is of course no reason why they should be expected to understand.

But, even after confessing their ignorance, such people often proceed to spout off, just as if they knew what they were talking about.

It is very easy for a pistol shot to miss, even in the safety and calm of a firing range, much less in a desperate situation where a decision must be made in a split second that can cost you your life or end someone else's life.

In a life-and-death situation, nobody counts how many bullets he is firing, much less how many bullets others are firing. It is not like a western movie, where the hero whips out his six-shooter, fires one time, and the villain drops dead.

A factual study of more than 200 real life incidents where the police fired their guns found that most of the shots missed.

Even at a distance as close as six feet, just over half the shots missed. This may be far less surprising to people who have actually fired pistols than to people who have not.

Not only can someone who is shooting a pistol for real not know beforehand whether or not his shots will hit the person who poses a danger, often it is not clear afterwards whether the shot hit anybody, depending on where it hit.

Nor does even a clear hit always render the wounded person harmless. When your life is on the line, you keep on firing until you are damn sure it is safe to stop.

Only afterwards does anybody count how many shots were fired. That is when the editorial office heroes give vent to their righteous indignation and their ignorant assumption that better "training" or better "rules" can solve the problem.

Such people seem to have no sense of the tragedy of the human condition, that there are times when decisions have to be made and acted upon immediately, whether or not we know as much as we would like to know or can carry out our decisions as perfectly as we wish we could.

People who are full of excuses for criminals— bad childhood, unemployment, unfair world— sit in the safety and comfort of their editorial offices and presume policemen to be guilty until proved innocent.

And they concoct clever headlines about killing an "unarmed" person, as if someone trying to run you over with a car poses no danger.

Where the person killed is black, as in the present case, that settles it, as far as the politically correct commentators are concerned, even though two of the three policemen who shot him are also black.

Not only do the people who put their lives on the line to protect the rest of us deserve better, we all deserve better than to have our own security undermined by those who undermine law enforcement. The police themselves can back off on law enforcement when irresponsible charges can ruin their careers and their lives. No one pays a higher price for that than low-income minority communities where crime flourishes.

Old Boxing Matches

Watching old boxing matches on DVDs tells us something about some of the ways in which American society has changed.

The first thing I noticed about the boxers back in the era of Joe Louis, from the 1930s into the 1950s, is that they all wore regulation boxing trunks and they didn't have tattoos. There was no trying to outdo each other with garish boxing trunks or wild tattoos. They didn't try to stare each other down when the referee was giving them instructions before the fight.

Seldom did any of these boxers go in for showboating during the fight. There was no denigrating the other fighter, either before or after the fight.

After Joe Louis knocked out an opponent, any comment he made was usually along the lines of "He's a good fighter and very game." Sometimes he would add, "He had me worried for a while," though there was seldom any real reason to worry.

One of the fighters who did give Joe Louis a real battle, and who was ahead on points when Louis knocked him out, was Billy Conn. But, when Conn lost his balance in their much anticipated rematch, Louis simply let him regain his balance before continuing the fight. How many boxers today would do that, especially against someone who was a real threat?

Although Joe Louis was widely respected as a model of sportsmanship, he was by no means the only one who behaved like a gentleman in the ring. That became a norm that heavyweight champions after him tried to live up to, until the 1960s.

Early in his career, Louis was upset by Max Schmeling, who knocked him out. Although Schmeling was from Germany and some tried to depict him as a Nazi, Schmeling went over to help Louis to his feet after the knockout.

In their rematch, the first thing Max Schmeling did upon entering the ring was go over to Louis' corner to shake hands with him, even before going to his own corner. It was a gesture that distanced him from the Aryan supremacy interpretation of his victory over Louis that the Nazi regime in Germany had made after their first fight.

The loutish, loudmouth and childish displays that have become all too common today in boxing, as well as in other sports, began in the 1960s, like so many other signs of social degeneration.

What about the quality of the fighters themselves? There have been great fighters in both earlier and later times. Mike Tyson's one-round knockouts electrified many boxing fans but Joe Louis still holds the record for one-round knockouts in heavyweight championship fights.

The only way you can be sure who hit harder would be to be on the receiving end of their punches— and none of the boxing pundits ever agreed to do that.

Louis' punches tended to be short and quick, but guys went down like they had been struck by lightning.

Cultural Issues

When Louis knocked out Jimmy Braddock— the "Cinderella Man"— to win the championship, Braddock lay face down on the canvas without moving while he was counted out, and afterwards his handlers had to come out from his corner to get him back on his feet.

It was much the same story when Rocky Marciano won the championship from Jersey Joe Walcott. After a right to the jaw from Marciano, Walcott fell limp. As he fell, his arm got tangled in the ropes, so that Walcott fell forward, with the top of his head resting on the canvas. He was counted out in that position without moving a muscle— and his handlers too had to come get him and revive him, before they could take him back to his corner.

How would the fighters of the past do against the bigger and heavier fighters of a later era? We will never know. What we do know is that Rocky Marciano, who was strictly a knockout fighter, never fought as heavy as 190 pounds and Joe Louis was at his best at no more than 200 pounds.

It is much easier to compare the referees. The old-timers didn't keep issuing warning after warning, for round after round. They penalized violations. More lax officiating may be why so many fights in recent times have had so many clinches and so much wrestling and dirty fighting.

That, too, is unfortunately a reflection of the general trends of our time.

The Right to Win

A mong the many new "rights" being conjured out of thin air, a new one seems to be a "right" to win.

Americans have long had the right to put their candidates and their ideas to a vote. Now there seems to be a sense that your rights have been trampled on if you don't win.

Hillary Clinton's supporters were not merely disappointed, but outraged, when she lost the Democrats' nomination to Barack Obama. Some took it as a sign that, while racial barriers had come down, the "glass ceiling" holding down women was still in place.

Apparently, if you don't win, somebody has put up a barrier or a ceiling. The more obvious explanation of the nomination outcome was that Obama ran a better campaign than Hillary. There is not the slightest reason to doubt that she would have been the nominee if the votes in the primaries had come out her way.

As the election approached, pundits warned that, if Obama lost, there would be riots in the ghetto. We will never know. But since when does any candidate have a right to win any office, much less the White House?

The worst of all the reactions from people who act as if they have a right to win have come from gay activists in the wake of voter rejection of so-called "gay marriage," which is to say, redefining what marriage has meant for centuries.

Blacks and Mormons have been the main targets of the gay activists' anger. Seventy percent of blacks voted against gay marriage in California, so racial epithets were hurled at blacks in Los Angeles— not in black neighborhoods, by the way.

Blacks who just happened to be driving through Westwood, near UCLA, were accosted in their cars and, in addition to being denounced, were warned, "You better watch your back."

Even blacks who were carrying signs in favor of gay marriage were denounced with racial epithets.

In Michigan, an evangelical church service was invaded and disrupted by gay activists, who also set off a fire alarm, because evangelicals had dared to exercise their right to express their opinions at the polls.

In Oakland, California, a mob gathered outside a Mormon temple in such numbers that officials shut down a nearby freeway exit for more than three hours.

In their midst was a San Francisco Supervisor who said, "The Mormon church has had to rely on our tolerance in the past, to be able to express their beliefs." He added, "This is a huge mistake for them. It looks like they've forgotten some lessons."

Apparently Mormons don't have the same rights as other Americans, at least not if they don't vote the way gay activists want them to vote.

There was another gay activist mob gathered outside a Mormon temple in Orange County, California.

In the past, gay activists have disrupted Catholic services and their "gay pride" parades in San Francisco have crudely mocked nuns.

While demanding tolerance from others, gay activists apparently feel no need to show any themselves.

How did we get to this kind of situation?

With all the various groups who act as if they have a right to win, we got to the present situation over the years, going back to the 1960s, where the idea started gaining acceptance that people who felt aggrieved don't have to follow the rules or even the law.

"No justice, no peace!" was a slogan that found resonance.

Like so many slogans, it sounds good if you don't stop and think— and awful if you do.

Almost by definition, everybody thinks their cause is just. Does that mean that nobody has to obey the rules? That is called anarchy.

Nobody is in favor of anarchy. But some people want everybody else to obey the rules, while they don't have to.

What they want is not decisive, however. It is what other people are willing to tolerate that determines how far any group can go. When the majority of the people become like sheep, who will tolerate intolerance rather than make a fuss, then there is no limit to how far any group will go.

Freedom and the Left

M ost people on the left are not opposed to freedom. They are just in favor of all sorts of things that are incompatible with freedom.

Freedom ultimately means the right of other people to do things that you do not approve of. Nazis were free to be Nazis under Hitler. It is only when you are able to do things that other people don't approve that you are free.

One of the most innocent-sounding examples of the left's many impositions of its vision on others is the widespread requirement by schools and by college admissions committees that students do "community service."

There are high schools across the country from which you cannot graduate, and colleges where your application for admission will not be accepted, unless you have engaged in activities arbitrarily defined as "community service."

The arrogance of commandeering young people's time, instead of leaving them and their parents free to decide for themselves how to use that time, is exceeded only by the arrogance of imposing your own notions as to what is or is not a service to the community.

Working in a homeless shelter is widely regarded as "community service"— as if aiding and abetting vagrancy is necessarily a service, rather than a disservice, to the community.

Is a community better off with more people not working, hanging out on the streets, aggressively panhandling people on the sidewalks, urinating in the street, leaving narcotics needles in the parks where children play?

This is just one of the ways in which handing out various kinds of benefits to people who have not worked for them breaks the connection between productivity and reward, as far as they are concerned.

But that connection remains as unbreakable as ever for society as a whole. You can make anything an "entitlement" for individuals and groups but nothing is an entitlement for society as a whole, not even food or shelter, both of which have to be produced by somebody's work or they will not exist.

What "entitlements" for some people mean is forcing other people to work for their benefit. As a bumper sticker put it: "Work harder. Millions of people on welfare are depending on you."

The most fundamental problem, however, is not which particular activities students are required to engage in under the title of "community service."

The most fundamental question is: What in the world qualifies teachers and members of college admissions committees to define what is good for society as a whole, or even for the students on whom they impose their arbitrary notions?

What expertise do they have that justifies overriding other people's freedom? What do their arbitrary impositions show, except that fools rush in where angels fear to tread?

What lessons do students get from this, except submission to arbitrary power?

Supposedly students are to get a sense of compassion or noblesse oblige from serving others. But this all depends on who defines compassion. In practice, it means forcing students to undergo a propaganda experience to make them receptive to the left's vision of the world.

I am sure those who favor "community service" requirements would understand the principle behind the objections to this if high school military exercises were required.

Indeed, many of those who promote compulsory "community service" activities are bitterly opposed to even voluntary military training in high schools or colleges, though many other people regard military training as more of a contribution to society than feeding people who refuse to work.

In other words, people on the left want the right to impose their idea of what is good for society on others—a right that they vehemently deny to those whose idea of what is good for society differs from their own.

The essence of bigotry is refusing to others the rights that you demand for yourself. Such bigotry is inherently incompatible with freedom, even though many on the left would be shocked to be considered opposed to freedom.

The Gratingest Generation

If our era could have its own coat of arms, it would be a yak against a background of mush. This must be the golden age of endless and pointless talk.

Every sports event seems to be preceded by all kinds of talk— whether by athletes repeating cliches that we have heard a thousand times, announcers making pseudo-profound sociological observations, or fans rambling on incoherently.

Then after the contest come the childish celebrations, the second-guessing and still more cliches.

Even when the action is going on at grand slam tennis matches, there are interviews with celebrities who happen to be in the stands, while the play on the court is ignored by both, even though it is shown on the screen.

Theatrical hype on the part of both the interviewer and the celebrity are common.

Does it ever occur to media chatterboxes that people watch tennis because they want to see tennis, not hear about some celebrity's latest movie or TV series?

If those who lived during World War II were "the greatest generation," this must be the gratingest generation.

It's not just the constant meaningless chatter that grates. There is the incessant self-dramatization.

Cultural Issues

Everybody knows about Manny Ramirez's hair styling. But there have been many other sluggers over the years, whose haircuts were never noticed. Does anyone remember Ted Williams' haircut or the haircuts of Mickey Mantle or Hank Aaron?

All those people are remembered for what they did, not how they looked.

Boxers and wrestlers must be the worst. Outlandish get-ups and behaving like badly raised brats have become the norm.

When you see old films of Joe Louis or Rocky Marciano, you see adults acting like adults— indeed, like gentlemen.

There was none of this making faces at an opponent before the fight or loudly boasting afterwards, much less taunting during the contest. In other words, you didn't have to act like a lout in order to be a boxer.

When Joe DiMaggio hit a ball that was caught up against the 415-foot sign in Yankee Stadium by a Dodger outfielder, at a crucial point during the 1947 World Series, DiMaggio briefly kicked the dirt in frustration while running the bases.

That was as close to an emotional outburst as DiMaggio ever came. That picture has been shown innumerable times, precisely because it was so exceptional for DiMaggio to go even that far.

Like so much that went wrong in American society, the new style of loutish self-dramatization began in the 1960s. When Muhammad Ali became heavyweight champion in 1964, it marked the end of the era when boxers simply did their job, collected their money and went home, usually after a few brief words.

Over the years, football players began carrying on with elaborate celebrations after every touchdown. Baseball teams developed pre-game rituals and post-game celebrations.

While this trend of self-dramatization is most visible in sports, it extends well beyond athletes.

Parents give their children off-the-wall names. "Mary" has long since lost its place as the perennially most popular name for girls.

There is a high turnover in what names are hot and which ones are not. Apparently everybody has to try to outdo everybody else, even when it comes to naming children.

Here, as in sports, superficial attention-getters have replaced achievements that speak for themselves. Indeed, the whole notion of achievement is downplayed, if not swept under the rug.

People who have achieved success are often referred to as "privileged," especially by the intelligentsia. Achievements used to be a source of inspiration for others but have been turned into a source of grievance for those without comparable achievements.

There have always been superficial dandies but they have not always been admired or regarded as models. Our society is worse off because they are.

The "Science" Mantra

S cience is one of the great achievements of the human mind and the biggest reason why we live not only longer but more vigorously in our old age, in addition to all the ways in which it provides us with things that make life easier and more enjoyable.

Like anything valuable, science has been seized upon by politicians and ideologues, and used to forward their own agendas. This started long ago, as far back as the 18th century, when the Marquis de Condorcet coined the term "social science" to describe various theories he favored. In the 19th century, Karl Marx and Friedrich Engels distinguished their own brand of socialism as "scientific socialism." By the 20th century, all sorts of notions wrapped themselves in the mantle of "science."

"Global warming" hysteria is only the latest in this long line of notions, whose main argument is that there is no argument, because it is "science." The recently revealed destruction of raw data at the bottom of the global warming hysteria, as well as revelations of attempts to prevent critics of this hysteria from being published in leading journals, suggests that the disinterested search for truth— the hallmark of real science— has taken a back seat to a political crusade.

An intercepted e-mail from a professor at the Climate Research Unit in England to a professor at the University of Pennsylvania warned the latter: "Don't any of you three tell anybody that the UK has a Freedom of Information Act" and urged the American professor to delete any e-mails he may have sent a colleague regarding the Intergovernmental Panel on Climate Change.

When a business accused of fraud begins shredding its memos and deleting its e-mails, the media are quick to proclaim these actions as signs of guilt. But, after the global warming advocates began a systematic destruction of evidence, the big television networks went for days without even reporting these facts, much less commenting on them.

As for politicians, Senator Barbara Boxer has urged prosecution of the hackers who uncovered and revealed the e-mails! People who have in the past applauded whistleblowers in business, in the military, or in Republican administrations, and who lionized the *New York Times* for publishing the classified Pentagon papers, are now shocked and outraged that someone dared to expose massive evidence of manipulations, concealment and destruction of data— and deliberate cover-ups of all this— in the global warming establishment.

Factual data are crucial in real science. Einstein himself urged that his own theory of relativity not be accepted until it could be empirically verified. This verification came when scientists around the world observed an eclipse of the sun and discovered that light behaved as Einstein's theory said it would behave, however implausible that might have seemed beforehand.

Today, politicized "science" has too big a stake in the global warming hysteria to let the facts speak for themselves and let the chips fall where they may. Too many people— in politics and in the media, as well as among those climate scientists who are promoting global warming hysteria— have too much at stake to let the raw data on which their calculations have been based fall into the "wrong hands."

People who talk about the corrupting influence of money seem to automatically assume that it is only private money that is corrupting. But, when governments have billions of dollars invested in the global warming crusade, massive programs underway and whole political careers at risk if that crusade gets undermined, do not expect the disinterested search for truth.

Among the intelligentsia, there have always been many who are ready to jump on virtually any bandwagon that will take them to the promised land, where the wise and noble few— like themselves— can take the rest of us poor dummies in hand and tell us how we had better change the way we live our lives.

No doubt some climate scientists honestly believe that global warming poses a threat. But other climate scientists honestly believe the opposite. That is why the raw data have had to be destroyed before the latter get their hands on it.

This is tragically the case as regards many other issues, besides global warming, where data are made available only to the true believers and kept out of the hands of those who think otherwise.

"Intellectuals"

Among the many wonders to be expected from an Obama administration, if Nicholas D. Kristof of the *New York Times* is to be believed, is ending "the anti-intellectualism that has long been a strain in American life."

He cited Adlai Stevenson, the suave and debonair governor of Illinois, who twice ran for president against Eisenhower in the 1950s, as an example of an intellectual in politics.

Intellectuals, according to Mr. Kristof, are people who are "interested in ideas and comfortable with complexity," people who "read the classics."

It is hard to know whether to laugh or cry.

Adlai Stevenson was certainly regarded as an intellectual by intellectuals in the 1950s. But, half a century later, facts paint a very different picture.

Historian Michael Beschloss, among others, has noted that Stevenson "could go quite happily for months or years without picking up a book." But Stevenson had the airs of an intellectual— the form, rather than the substance.

What is more telling, form was enough to impress the intellectuals, not only then but even now, years after the facts have been revealed, though apparently not to Mr. Kristof. That is one of many reasons why intellectuals are not taken as seriously by others as they take themselves.

As for reading the classics, President Harry Truman, whom no one thought of as an intellectual, was a voracious reader of heavyweight stuff like Thucydides and read Cicero in the original Latin. When Chief Justice Fred Vinson quoted in Latin, Truman was able to correct him.

Yet intellectuals tended to think of the unpretentious and plain-spoken Truman as little more than a country bumpkin.

Similarly, no one ever thought of President Calvin Coolidge as an intellectual. Yet Coolidge also read the classics in the White House. He read both Latin and Greek, and read Dante in the original Italian, since he spoke several languages. It was said that the taciturn Coolidge could be silent in five different languages.

The intellectual levels of politicians are just one of the many things that intellectuals have grossly misjudged for years on end.

During the 1930s, some of the leading intellectuals in America condemned our economic system and pointed to the centrally planned Soviet economy as a model— all this at a time when literally millions of people were starving to death in the Soviet Union, from a famine in a country with some of the richest farmland in Europe and historically a large exporter of food.

New York Times Moscow correspondent Walter Duranty won a Pulitzer Prize for telling the intelligentsia what they wanted to hear— that claims of starvation in the Ukraine were false.

After British journalist Malcolm Muggeridge reported from the Ukraine on the massive deaths from starvation there, he was ostracized after returning to England and unable to find a job.

More than half a century later, when the archives of the Soviet Union were finally opened up under Mikhail Gorbachev, it turned out that about six million people had died in that famine— about the same number as the people killed in Hitler's Holocaust.

In the 1930s, it was the intellectuals who pooh-poohed the dangers from the rise of Hitler and urged Western disarmament.

It would be no feat to fill a big book with all the things on which intellectuals were grossly mistaken, just in the 20th century— far more so than ordinary people.

History fully vindicates the late William F. Buckley's view that he would rather be ruled by people represented by the first 100 names in the Boston phone book than by the faculty of Harvard.

How have intellectuals managed to be so wrong, so often? By thinking that because they are knowledgeable— or even expert— within some narrow band out of the vast spectrum of human concerns, that makes them wise guides to the masses and to the rulers of the nation.

But the ignorance of Ph.D.s is still ignorance and high-IQ groupthink is still groupthink, which is the antithesis of real thinking.

Autism Cures?

"New Ways to Diagnose Autism Earlier" read a recent headline in the *Wall Street Journal*. There is no question that you can diagnose anything as early as you want. The real question is whether the diagnosis will turn out to be correct.

My own awareness of how easy it is to make false diagnoses of autism grew out of experiences with a group of parents of late-talking children that I formed back in 1993.

A number of those children were diagnosed as autistic. But the passing years have shown most of the diagnoses to have been false, as most of these children have not only begun talking but have developed socially.

Some parents have even said, "Now I wish he would shut up."

I did absolutely nothing to produce these results. As a layman, I refused to diagnose these children, much less suggest any treatment, even though many parents wanted such advice.

As word of my group spread, various parents would write to ask if they could bring their child to me to seek my impression or advice. I declined every time.

Yet, if I had concocted some half-baked method of diagnosing and treating these children, I could now claim a high rate of success in "curing" autism, based on case studies. Perhaps my success rate would be as high as that claimed by various programs being touted in the media.

If a child is not autistic to begin with, almost anything will "cure" him with the passage of time.

My work brought me into contact with Professor Stephen Camarata of Vanderbilt University, who has specialized in the study of late-talking children— and who is qualified to diagnose autism.

Professor Camarata has organized his own group of parents of late-talking children, which has grown to hundreds, as compared to the several dozen children in my group. Yet the kinds of children and the kinds of families are remarkably similar in the two groups, in ways spelled out in my book *The Einstein Syndrome*.

The difference is that Professor Camarata is not a layman but a dedicated professional, with decades of experience— and he too has expressed dismay at the number of false diagnoses of autism that he has encountered.

What Camarata has also encountered is something that I encountered in my smaller group— parents who have been told to allow their child to be diagnosed as autistic, in order to become eligible for government money that is available, and can be used for speech therapy or whatever other treatment the child might need.

How much this may have contributed to the soaring statistics on the number of children diagnosed as autistic is something that nobody knows— and apparently not many people are talking about it.

Another factor in the great increase in the number of children diagnosed as autistic is a growing practice of referring to children as being on "the autistic spectrum."

In other words, a child may not actually be autistic but has a number of characteristics common among autistic children. The problem with this approach is that lots of children who are not autistic have characteristics that are common among autistic children.

For example, a study of high-IQ children by Professor Ellen Winner of Boston College found these children to have "obsessive interests" and "often play alone and enjoy solitude," as well as being children who "seem to march to their own drummer" and have "prodigious memories." Many of the children in my group and in Professor Camarata's group have these characteristics.

Those who diagnose children by running down a checklist of "symptoms" can find many apparently "autistic" children or children on "the autism spectrum."

Parents need to be spared the emotional trauma of false diagnoses and children need to be spared stressful treatments that follow false diagnoses. Yet the "autism spectrum" concept provides lots of wiggle room for those who are making false diagnoses.

Real autism may not get as much money as it needs if much of that money is dissipated on children who are not in fact autistic.

But money is money to those who are running research projects— and a gullible media helps them get that money.

All the "News"?

The latest in a long line of *New York Times* editorials disguised as "news" stories was a recent article suggesting that most American women today do not have husbands. Partly this was based on Census data— but much more so on creative definitions.

The *Times* defined "women" to include females as young as sixteen and counted widows, who of course could not be widows unless they had once had a husband. Wives whose husbands were away in the military, or in prison, were also counted among women not living with a husband.

With such creative definitions, it turned out that 51 percent of "women" were not living with a husband. That made it "most" women and created a "news" story suggesting that these women were not married. In reality, only one fourth of women have never married, even when you count girls as young as sixteen.

While the data quoted in the *New York Times* story were about women who were not living with a husband, there were quotes in the story about women who rejected marriage.

What was the point? To show that marriage is a thing of the past. As a headline in the *San Francisco Chronicle* put it: "Women See Less Need for Ol' Ball and Chain."

Cultural Issues

In other words, marriage is like a prison sentence, complete with the old fashioned leg irons with a chain connected to a heavy metal ball, so that the prisoner cannot escape.

This picture of marriage and a family as a burden is not peculiar to the *New York Times* or the *San Francisco Chronicle*. It is common among the intelligentsia of the left.

Negative depictions of marriage and family are common not only in our newspapers but also wherever the left is concentrated, whether in our schools and colleges or on television or in the movies— most famously, in the "Murphy Brown" TV program that Vice President Dan Quayle criticized, provoking a fierce counterattack from the left.

The *New York Times* was not the first outlet of the left to play fast and loose with statistics in order to depict marriage as a relic of the past. Innumerable sources have quoted a statistic that half of all marriages end in divorce— another conclusion based on creative manipulation of words, rather than on hard facts.

The fact that there may be half as many divorces in a given year as there are marriages in that year does not mean that half of all marriages end in divorce.

It is completely misleading to compare all the divorces in one year— from marriages begun years and even decades earlier— with the number of marriages begun in that one year.

Why these desperate twistings of words and numbers by the left, in order to discredit marriage?

Partly it is because marriage is a fundamental component of a social order that the left opposes.

Moreover, marriage is seen as one of the social restrictions on individual free choice.

These are not new ideas, even though they may be more pervasive than in the past, simply because the intelligentsia is larger and more vocal today.

As far back as the 18th century, Rousseau said that man is born free but is everywhere in chains. In other words, the social restrictions essential to a civilized society were seen as unnecessary hindrances to each individual's freedom.

It never seems to occur to those who think this way that if everyone were free of all social restrictions, only the strongest and most ruthless would in fact be free, and all the others would be subject to their dictates or destruction.

Marriage and family are also barriers to the left's desire to create a society built to their own specifications. Friedrich Engels' first draft of *The Communist Manifesto* proclaimed the end of families, but Karl Marx thought better of it and took that out.

In one way or another, however, the left has for more than two centuries tried to undermine families— including today redefining the words "marriage" and "family" to include whatever kind of people want to live together in whatever way for whatever reason.

If "marriage" can mean anything, then it means nothing.

The *New York Times*' long-standing motto, "All the News That's Fit to Print" should be changed to reflect today's reality: "Manufacturing News to Fit an Ideology."

Myths of '68

This 40th anniversary of the turbulent year of 1968 is already starting to spawn nostalgic accounts of that year that we can look for during this year in articles and books, especially by aging 1960s radicals seeking to relive their youth.

The events of 1968 have continuing implications for our times but not the implications drawn by those with romantic myths about 1968 and about themselves.

The first of the shocks of 1968 was the sudden eruption of violent attacks by Communist guerillas in the cities of South Vietnam, known as the "Tet offensive," after a local holiday.

That this sort of widespread urban guerilla warfare was still possible, after the rosy claims of American officials in Washington and Vietnam, sent shock waves through the United States.

The conclusion that might have been drawn was that politicians and military commanders should not make rosy predictions. The conclusion that was in fact drawn was that the Vietnam war was unwinnable.

In reality, the Tet offensive was one in which the Communist guerilla movement was not only defeated in battle but was virtually annihilated as a major military force. From there on, the job of attacking South Vietnam was a job for the North Vietnam army.

Politically, however, the Tet offensive was an enormous victory for the Communists— not in Vietnam, but in the United States.

The American media pictured the Tet offensive as a defeat for the United States and a sign that the Vietnam war was unwinnable.

That in turn led to the second shock of 1968, President Lyndon Johnson's announcement that he would not run for re-election. He knew that public support for the war was completely undermined— and that is what in fact made the war politically unwinnable.

Think about it: More than 50,000 Americans gave their lives to win victories on the battlefields of Vietnam that were thrown away back in the United States by the media, by politicians and by rioters in the streets and on campus.

Years later, Communist leaders in Vietnam admitted that they had not defeated the United States militarily in Vietnam but politically in the United States.

The next great shock of 1968 was the assassination of Martin Luther King, Jr. The after-shocks included the riots that swept through black ghettos across the country.

These orgies of mass destruction, vandalism, looting and deaths have likewise been seen nostalgically as mass "uprisings" against "the system."

But "the system" did not kill Martin Luther King. An assassin did. And the biggest losers from the 1968 riots were the black communities in which they occurred.

Many of those communities have never recovered to this day from the massive loss of businesses and jobs.

Cultural Issues

Then came the next great shock of 1968: The assassination of Robert F. Kennedy. Deep thinkers tried to claim that somehow it was America that was in some way responsible for these assassinations. In reality, the assassin of Robert Kennedy was not an American, but was from the Middle East.

Dispersed among these national shocks were various local and regional shocks, as colleges and universities across the country were hit by student disruptions and violence of one sort or another over one issue or another.

Like the urban ghetto riots, campus riots flourished where the authorities failed to use their authority to preserve order. Instead, academics sought to cleverly finesse the issues with negotiations, concessions and mealy-mouthed expressions of "understanding" of the concerns raised by rioters.

Many academics congratulated themselves on the eventual restoration of calm to campuses in the 1970s. But it was the calm of surrender. The terms of surrender included creation of whole departments devoted to ideological indoctrination.

Many academics see the kind of negotiations and concessions they engaged in during the 1960s as a pattern to be followed by the United States in the international arena. Whatever they may choose to call it, it is in fact surrender on the instalment plan.

Say It Ain't So

S hoeless Joe Jackson was the only man to bat .382 in his last season in the major leagues. After that he was banned for life for his role in the "Black Sox scandal," the deliberate throwing of the 1919 World Series.

It was to Jackson that a youngster was supposed to have said, "Say it ain't so, Joe."

Maybe we are too sophisticated today to react that way to the news that many major league star players have been taking steroids or other performance-enhancing drugs. But maybe we have gotten too sophisticated for our own good.

Some people are questioning whether there should now be asterisks alongside the records of Barry Bonds or other star players. That is the least of the problems— and the least of the solutions.

Steroids are dangerous and sometimes fatal. Yet, if some players use them, others will feel the pressure to use them as well, in order to compete.

Most important of all, many young people will imitate their sports heroes— and pay the price. Those young people are far more important than asterisks.

You might think that athletes who are making a million dollars— not per year, but sometimes per month— could spare some concern for the kids who look up to them.

But too many think only of themselves, and not always wisely, even for themselves.

Football star Michael Vick's downfall was dog-fighting, rather than steroids, but it was the same reckless disregard of rules, jeopardizing a career that would have earned him more in a few years than most people make in a lifetime.

Even those of us who are not Michael Vick fans have to find it painful to see a young man self-destruct this way. If anything good comes out of this, it might be that his fate may deter others.

The bottom line question for those in authority, whether in the courts or in professional sports is, "What are you going to do about it?"

The law has already spoken in the case of Michael Vick. It is too early to say what the law will do in the case of Barry Bonds and others involved in the steroid controversy.

But it is not too early to point out that what the law does or does not do is separate from what the people in charge of professional sports do.

In a court of law, the accused is presumed to be "innocent until proven guilty" beyond a reasonable doubt. But too many people mindlessly repeat that phrase for things outside of courts.

All the ballplayers accused of throwing the 1919 World Series were acquitted in a court of law— and all were nevertheless banned from baseball for life anyway by the commissioner of baseball.

In a sense, that ban applied not only for life but beyond death. None of those players has been put in the Baseball Hall of Fame, even though Shoeless Joe

Jackson hit .408 at his peak and left a lifetime batting average of .356.

That was long before we became so sophisticated that we learned to come up with excuses for those who violate rules and additional excuses for those who refuse to impose penalties.

Today there are those who lament Pete Rose's exclusion from the Baseball Hall of Fame, despite a record on the field that would certainly have put him there, except for breaking rules.

But Shoeless Joe Jackson's even more impressive record would certainly have put him in Cooperstown, if he had not broken the rules.

There is still some lingering hope of sanity in the baseball writers' refusal to vote Mark McGwire into the Baseball Hall of Fame, despite his tremendous career achievements.

Keeping known rule-breakers out of Cooperstown would be a lot more effective deterrent than putting asterisks alongside their records, to be disregarded by those who are "non-judgmental."

Unfortunately Senator George Mitchell's report on steroid use in the major leagues and its recommendations are of the let-bygones-be-bygones approach that has spread the disregard of rules throughout the whole society, from student cheaters to career criminals.

Preserving a Vision

In Shelby Steele's book, *White Guilt*, he mentions an encounter with a white liberal who fiercely defended the welfare state programs and policies of the 1960s:

"Damn it, we *saved* this country!" he all but shouted. "This country was about to blow up. There were riots everywhere. You can stand there now in hindsight and criticize, but we had to keep the country together, my friend."

Before we turn to facts, we need to understand the vision. This is a vision of the world more precious than gold. To those who believe it, this vision is a treasure beyond price because it is also a wonderful vision of themselves— and they are not likely to give it up for anything so mundane as grubby facts.

For those liberals who lived through the 1960s, that was often also the springtime of their youth, increasingly treasured as a memory, as the grim realities of old age settle down upon them today. It is expecting an awful lot to expect them to consider any alternative vision of the world, especially one that shatters the beautiful picture of themselves as wise and compassionate saviors of society.

But what are the facts?

While liberals may think of the 1960s as the beginning of many "progressive" trends in American society, cold hard facts tell a very different story. The

1960s marked the end of many beneficial trends that had been going on for years— and a complete reversal of those trends as programs, policies, and ideologies of the liberals took hold.

Teenage pregnancy had been going down for years. So had venereal disease. The rate of infection for syphilis in 1960 was half of what it had been in 1950. There were similar trends in crime. The total number of murders in the United States in 1960 was lower than in 1950, 1940, or 1930— even though the population was growing over those years and two new states had been added. The murder rate, in proportion to population, in 1960 was half of what it had been in 1934.

Every one of these beneficial trends sharply reversed after liberal notions gained ascendancy during the 1960s. By 1974, the murder rate had doubled. Even liberal icon Sargent Shriver, head of the agency directing the "war on poverty," admitted that "venereal disease has skyrocketed" even though "we have had more clinics, more pills, and more sex education than ever in history."

Liberals looking back on the 1960s take special pride in their role on racial issues, for civil rights laws and the advancement of blacks out of poverty. Those riots that threatened to tear the country apart were race riots— and supposedly the liberals saved us all.

But what do the facts show?

Both the Civil Rights Act of 1964 and the Voting Rights Act of 1965 had a higher percentage of Congressional Republicans voting for their enactment than the percentage of Congressional Democrats. You can check it out in *The Congressional Record.*

Cultural Issues

As for black economic advances, the most dramatic reduction in poverty among blacks occurred between 1940 and 1960, when the black poverty rate was cut almost in half, without any major government programs of the Great Society kind that began in the 1960s. Liberals love to point to the rise of blacks out of poverty since 1960 as proof of the benefits of liberal programs, as if the continuation of a trend that began decades earlier was proof of how liberals saved blacks.

As for saving the country from riots, the facts show the direct opposite. It was precisely when liberals were in power that riots rocked cities across the country. There were never as many riots during the two presidential terms of Ronald Reagan as during one term of Lyndon Johnson.

Even during the 1960s, riots were far more common and deadly in liberal bastions like New York City than in Chicago, where the original Mayor Daley announced on television that he had given his police orders to "shoot to kill" if riots broke out.

Daley was demonized for saying such a thing, even though Chicago did not have the loss of life suffered in liberal cities where mayors pandered to grievance-mongers and pleaded for restraint. In other words, the net effect was that Daley saved lives while liberals saved their vision.

LEGAL ISSUES

Since no society can continue to exist indefinitely in anarchy, there must be law— a set of rules backed by power, providing a skeletal structure that supports and holds together the many disparate parts of a complex society. Yet the history of human beings individually, and of whole nations, is painfully full of abuses of power, in ways large and small— and sometimes in ways fatal to a whole society, when law collapses and gives way to either anarchy or arbitrary tyranny.

Legal issues are not just a matter of how one feels about particular individuals or particular policy issues, viewed in isolation. What is crucially at stake when courts wrestle with the fate of particular individuals, institutions or policies is the fate of law itself. It is all too easy to get so involved and invested in the outcomes for individuals, institutions or policies, as to lose sight of how the legal *process* itself can become compromised or corrupted while preoccupied with reaching particular results.

This is all too plain— and painful— when a prosecutor brings the full weight of the law crashing down on particular individuals, with little or no regard for whether there was even a crime committed by anybody, in the first place. Two, among all too many examples, are covered in columns in this section about such prosecutions of Lewis "Scooter" Libby in Washington or three Duke University students in North Carolina.

The Duke "rape" case was covered in a number of my columns, over a period of a year, only four of which are reproduced here. This extensive coverage was because that case revealed a moral dry rot that extended far beyond the legal system and included both the media and academia as major contributors to a frenzied lynch mob atmosphere, in which anyone who dared to doubt the guilt of the three accused young men was treated as a moral leper. Yet the strange procedures of the prosecutor from the outset gave ample evidence of the fraudulence of the case, as I pointed out in my first column on this case, a year before the multiple layers of fraudulence were exposed by the state attorney general, forcing the resignation of District Attorney Michael Nifong and his subsequent disbarment.

This is not just the story of one man's misuse of the law. It is a story of whole institutions and movements that generated a lynch mob atmosphere which threatened the integrity of the law itself, in addition to threatening to ruin the lives of three young men, who could not be guilty of a crime that had not been committed. Among the most disturbing e-mails I received during the year that I wrote about the Duke "rape" case were e-mails that asked why I was so concerned about "three rich white guys." That attitude is more of a threat to the integrity of the law than even a corrupt prosecutor. Indeed, it is a threat to a whole society, for a society cannot remain a society if it degenerates into a war of each against all.

Prosecutorial misconduct is just one of the many threats to the integrity of the law. Judges who treat the law as simply a grant of arbitrary power to themselves, to impose their pet notions on individuals, institutions or a whole society, have an even wider scope for lawlessness in the name of law. Here, too, it is the general atmosphere in society at large that allows this corruption of the law to flourish. The Senate has the power to impeach judges and remove them from the bench but, as a matter of political reality, that power cannot be exercised in an atmosphere in which "the rule of law" is confused with the rule of judges.

Those who see court decisions as simply a means to their particular ends— whether on issues like abortion or gun control, or innumerable other issues— are treating the integrity of the law as expendable, when law is what holds a society together. Here, too, it is all too easy to start down the slippery slope that leads to the war of each against all.

The cry of "No justice, no peace!" is a cry that may find resonance among those who do not see beyond the issue of the moment. But, since there are innumerable and conflicting notions of what is or is not justice, it is a cry for the disregard of laws by people in any part of the ideological spectrum— which is to say, it is a cry for a war of each against all. Like other erosions and violations of the integrity of law, such a cry is magnified by the support or acquiescence of many people and institutions in the larger society.

The more people who see the law as simply a means to their own particular ends, the more the whole framework on which we all depend is in danger of being dismantled, as part of the general dismantling of America.

"Empathy" versus Law

I t is one of the signs of our times that so many in the media are focusing on the life story of Judge Sonia Sotomayor, President Obama's nominee for the Supreme Court of the United States.

You might think that this was some kind of popularity contest, instead of a weighty decision about someone whose impact on the fundamental law of the nation will extend for decades after Barack Obama has come and gone.

Much is being made of the fact that Sonia Sotomayor had to struggle to rise in the world. But stop and think.

If you were going to have open heart surgery, would you want to be operated on by a surgeon who was chosen because he had to struggle to get where he is or by the best surgeon you could find— even if he was born with a silver spoon in his mouth and had every advantage that money and social position could offer?

If it were you who was going to be lying on that operating table with his heart cut open, you wouldn't give a tinker's damn about somebody's struggle or somebody else's privileges.

The Supreme Court of the United States is in effect operating on the heart of our nation— the Constitution and the statutes and government policies that all of us must live under.

Barack Obama's repeated claim that a Supreme Court justice should have "empathy" with various groups has raised red flags that we ignore at our peril—and at the peril of our children and grandchildren.

"Empathy" for particular groups can be reconciled with "equal justice under law"— the motto over the entrance to the Supreme Court— only with smooth words. But not in reality. President Obama used those smooth words in introducing Judge Sotomayor but words do not change realities.

Nothing demonstrates the fatal dangers from judicial "empathy" more than Judge Sotomayor's decision in a 2008 case involving firemen who took an exam for promotion. After the racial mix of those who passed that test turned out to be predominantly white, with only a few blacks and Hispanics, the results were thrown out.

When this action by the local civil service authorities was taken to court and eventually reached the 2nd Circuit Court of Appeals, Judge Sotomayor did not give the case even the courtesy of a spelling out of the issues. She backed those who threw out the test results. Apparently she didn't have "empathy" with those predominantly white males who had been cheated out of promotions they had earned.

Fellow 2nd Circuit Court judge Jose Cabranes commented on the short shrift given to the serious issues in this case. It so happens that he too is Hispanic, but apparently he does not decide legal issues on the basis of "empathy" or lack thereof.

This was not an isolated matter for Judge Sotomayor. Speaking at the University of California at Berkeley in

2001, she said that the ethnicity and sex of a judge "may and will make a difference in our judging."

Moreover, this was not something she lamented. On the contrary, she added, "I would hope that a wise Latina woman with the richness of her experiences would more often than not reach a better conclusion than a white male who hasn't lived that life."

No doubt the political spinmasters will try to spin this to mean something innocent. But the cold fact is that this is a poisonous doctrine for any judge, much less a justice of the Supreme Court.

That kind of empathy would for all practical purposes repeal the 14th Amendment to the Constitution of the United States, which guarantees "equal protection of the laws" to all Americans.

What would the political spinmasters say if some white man said that a white male would more often reach a better conclusion than a Hispanic female?

For those who believe in the rule of law, Barack Obama used the words "rule of law" in introducing his nominee. For those who take his words as gospel, even when his own actions are directly the opposite of his words, that may be enough to let him put this dangerous woman on the Supreme Court.

Even if her confirmation cannot be stopped, it is important for Senators to warn of the dangers, which will only get worse if such nominations sail through the Senate smoothly.

"Empathy" versus Law: Part II

The great Supreme Court justice Oliver Wendell Holmes is not the kind of justice who would have been appointed under President Barack Obama's criterion of "empathy" for certain groups.

Like most people, Justice Holmes had empathy for some and antipathy for others, but his votes on the Supreme Court often went against those for whom he had empathy and for those for whom he had antipathy. As Holmes himself put it: "I loathed most of the things in favor of which I decided."

After voting in favor of Benjamin Gitlow in the 1925 case of *Gitlow v. People of New York*, Holmes said in a letter to a friend that he had just voted for "the right of an ass to drool about proletarian dictatorship." Similarly, in the case of *Abrams v. United States*, Holmes' dissenting opinion in favor of the appellants characterized the views of those appellants as "a creed which I believe to be the creed of ignorance and immaturity."

By the same token, Justice Holmes did not let his sympathies with some people determine his votes on the High Court. As a young man, Holmes had dropped out of Harvard to go fight in the Civil War because he opposed slavery. In later years, he expressed his dislike of the minstrel shows that were popular at the time "because they seem to belittle the race."

When there were outcries against the prosecution of Sacco and Vanzetti in the 1920s, Holmes said in a letter, "I cannot but ask myself why this so much greater interest in red than black. A thousand-fold worse cases of negroes come up from time to time, but the world does not worry over them."

Yet when two black attorneys appeared before the Supreme Court, Holmes wrote in another letter to a friend that he had to "write a decision against a very thorough and really well expressed argument by two colored men"— an argument "that even in intonation was better than, I should say, the majority of white discourses that we hear."

Holmes understood that a Supreme Court justice was not there to favor some people or even to prescribe what was best for society. He had a very clear sense of what the role of a judge was— and wasn't.

Justice Holmes saw his job to be "to see that the game is played according to the rules whether I like them or not."

That was because the law existed for the citizens, not for lawyers or judges, and the citizens had to know what the rules were, in order to obey them.

He said: "Men should know the rules by which the game is played. Doubt as to the value of some of those rules is no sufficient reason why they should not be followed by the courts."

Legislators existed to change the law.

After a lunch with Judge Learned Hand, as Holmes was departing in a carriage to return to work, Judge Hand said to him: "Do justice, sir. Do justice."

Holmes had the carriage stopped. "That is not my job," he said. "My job is to apply the law."

Holmes wrote that he did not "think it desirable that the judges should undertake to renovate the law." If the law needed changing, that was what the democratic process was for. Indeed, that was what the separation of powers in legislative, executive and judicial branches by the Constitution of the United States was for.

"The criterion of constitutionality," he said, "is not whether we believe the law to be for the public good." That was for other people to decide. For judges, he said: "When we know what the source of the law has said it shall be, our authority is at an end."

One of Holmes' judicial opinions ended: "I am not at liberty to consider the justice of the Act."

Some have tried to depict Justice Holmes as someone who saw no need for morality in the law. On the contrary, he said: "The law is the witness and external deposit of our moral life." But a society's need to put moral content into its laws did not mean that it was the judge's job to second-guess the moral choices made by others who were authorized to make such choices.

Justice Holmes understood the difference between the rule of law and the rule of lawyers and judges.

The Legal Meatgrinder

I f you wanted a textbook example of what is wrong about appointing a special prosecutor, the prosecution of White House aide Lewis "Scooter" Libby is a classic. Let's go back to square one to see how this sorry chapter in criminal law unfolded.

The charge that was trumpeted through the media was that the Bush administration had leaked the fact that Joe Wilson's wife worked for the C.I.A. in retaliation against him for saying that Saddam Hussein was not seeking uranium in Niger, contrary to intelligence reports cited as one of the reasons for invading Iraq.

Since there is a law against revealing the identity of a C.I.A. agent, a great hue and cry went up for a special prosecutor to find and prosecute whoever leaked that information.

Some in the media gleefully anticipated seeing White House adviser Karl Rove, or perhaps even Vice President Dick Cheney, being frog-marched out of the White House in handcuffs.

Attorney General John Ashcroft appointed a special prosecutor, Patrick Fitzgerald, to investigate these charges.

Here is where the story takes a strange and disturbing twist. Today we know what we did not know when it happened— namely, that Fitzgerald discovered early on that the leaker was not any of the White House officials on whom suspicion was focussed.

It was Richard Armitage in the State Department. Moreover, Joe Wilson's wife had a desk job at the C.I.A., and revealing that fact was not a violation of the criminal law.

In other words, there was no crime to prosecute and there was no mystery to solve as to who had leaked Wilson's wife's name to columnist Robert Novak.

At this point, a regular prosecutor would have decided that he had other things to do than to pursue an investigation of a non-mystery about a non-crime. But special prosecutors are different.

Patrick Fitzgerald insisted on keeping the investigation going for three years— and keeping secret the fact that there was no crime involved and no mystery about who leaked.

In the course of this pointless investigation, it turned out that some of Scooter Libby's statements conflicted with the statements of some reporters. So Libby was prosecuted for perjury and obstruction of justice— and a Washington jury convicted him.

Not only did Libby's recollections differ from that of some reporters, some of those reporters differed among themselves as to what had been said and some differed in their later testimony from what they had said in their earlier testimony.

The information about Joe Wilson's wife was so incidental and trivial at the time that it is hardly surprising that it was not fixed in people's minds as something memorable. Only later hype in the media made it look big.

With Libby handling heavy duties in the White House, there is no reason for his memory to be expected to be better than that of others about something like this— much less to convict him of perjury.

As for the pay-back conspiracy theory of a Bush administration-inspired leak because of Wilson's opposition to the Iraq war, Richard Armitage was not an Iraq war hawk and columnist Robert Novak opposed the war. They had no reason to discredit Wilson.

Even the term "leak" is misleading. In the course of a discussion, Novak simply asked Armitage why someone with no expertise like Joe Wilson had been sent to Niger in the first place— and Armitage's answer was that he was sent at the suggestion of his wife, who worked at the C.I.A.

Novak's column was not about that fact but mentioned it in passing. From this the liberal media went ballistic with conspiracy theories that we now know were totally false.

A man's life has been ruined because his memories differed from that of others— whose memories also differed among themselves— and media liberals are exulting as if their conspiracy theories had been vindicated.

More important, how are we to expect highly qualified people, with far better options than a government job, to risk being put through the Washington meatgrinder because of politics, media hype and special prosecutors who can create crimes in the course of an investigation, when there was none to begin with?

Supreme Farce

It might be a hilarious comedy routine to have a group of highly educated judges solemnly expounding on something that everybody knows to be utter nonsense. But it isn't nearly as funny when this solemn discourse about nonsense takes place on the Supreme Court of the United States— and when most people are unaware of what nonsense the learned justices are talking.

The issue before the High Court is whether local authorities have the legal right to make students' race a factor in deciding which school to assign them to attend.

The parent of a white student is complaining because he is not allowed to go to the school near where he lives but is instead being assigned to a different school far away, in order to create the kind of racial mix of students the local authorities are seeking, in the name of "diversity."

Those of us old enough to remember the landmark 1954 Supreme Court decision in *Brown v. Board of Education* will see a painful irony now, since that case began because a black girl was not allowed to go to a school near where she lived but was instead assigned to a different school far away, because of the prevailing racial dogmas of that day.

The racial dogmas have changed since 1954 but they are still dogmas. And flesh-and-blood children are still being sacrificed on the altar to those dogmas.

Some of the learned justices are pondering whether there is a "compelling" government interest in creating the educational and social benefits of racial "diversity." If so, then supposedly it is OK to do to white kids today what the Supreme Court back in 1954 said could not be done to black kids— namely, assign children to schools according to their race.

What are those "compelling" benefits of "diversity"? They are as invisible as the proverbial emperor's new clothes. Yet everyone has to pretend to believe in those benefits, as they pretended to admire the naked emperor's wardrobe.

Not only is there no hard evidence that mixing and matching black and white kids in school produces either educational or social benefits, there have been a number of studies of all-black schools whose educational performances equal or exceed the national average, even though most black schools fall far below the average.

My own study of successful all-black schools was published more than 30 years ago in *The Public Interest* quarterly. Since then, there have been other studies of similar schools across the country, published by the Heritage Foundation in Washington and by scholars Abigail and Stephan Thernstrom, among others.

There have also been all-Chinese-American schools that exceeded national norms. How have such schools managed to succeed and excel without the "compelling" need for a racial mixing of students?

Look at it another way: Have black kids bussed into white schools had their test scores shoot up? No— not even after decades of bussing.

Some black students— in fact, whole schools of them— have performed dramatically better than other black students and exceeded the norms in white schools.

Yet this phenomenon, which goes back as far as 1899 and included an all-black school within walking distance of the Supreme Court that declared such things impossible back in 1954, is totally ignored.

Are such things exceptional? Yes. But the mystical benefits of "diversity" are non-existent, however politically correct it is to proclaim such benefits.

Hard evidence shows that students of all races can succeed or fail in schools that are racially mixed or racially unmixed.

The latest variation on the theme of mixing and matching by race is that there needs to be a "critical mass" of black students in a given school or college, in order for them to perform up to standard.

Not only is there no hard evidence for this dogma, such hard evidence as there is points in the opposite direction. Bright black kids have benefitted from being in classes with other bright kids, regardless of the other kids' color.

All this is ignored in the Supreme Court's supreme farce.

The Left and Crime

Oakland, California, continues to suffer the high crime rate, and especially the high murder rate, which has long afflicted that city. Judging by a recent speech by its current mayor, long-time leftist Ron Dellums, it can look forward to a future all too much like its past.

Why is Oakland so crime-ridden? According to Mayor Dellums, "we have closed our eyes to the injustices and inequities, and now we are reaping the wild winds of that disregard for a whole range of people."

This is the "root causes of crime" rhetoric of the 1960s, still going strong on the left today, despite mountains of evidence to the contrary that have accumulated in the decades since then.

That is what makes Oakland's problem more than just Oakland's problem— or even America's problem. The same kind of thinking prevails on the left in other countries, producing the same kinds of dire results.

As British writer Peter Hitchens put it: "England is rapidly becoming a place where the good are afraid of the bad and the bad are not afraid of anything."

He also said, "The sheer concrete-headed stupidity of most political statements about crime defies belief." Both statements would apply as much in Oakland as they do in London— and in many other places in between.

A newspaper account of Oakland mayor Ron Dellums' speech said that he was "clearly comfortable with what he was conveying and speaking without notes."

Why should he be uncomfortable or need notes to be repeating the same politically correct notions that the entire left— here and overseas— has been repeating like a mantra for nearly half a century? Would you need notes to recite the alphabet?

The idea that "injustices and inequities" explain crime goes back more than two centuries. You can find it in William Godwin's 1793 book, *Enquiry Concerning Political Justice* in England and even earlier in a number of writers in France.

It is the hallmark of the left around the world.

While such ideas have been around for centuries, they did not become the dominant ideas among those making legal and political policy until the second half of the 20th century— more specifically, the 1960s in the United States.

What was crime like in 1960, before these ideas took over in our courts and in the legislative and executive branches of government?

As of 1960, the murder rate had been going down for decades— among blacks and whites alike— and was just under half of what it had been back in 1934.

Were there no "injustices and inequities" in 1960 and in the prior decades? No one who is old enough to remember those times could believe that.

It was precisely the rise to power in the 1960s (in the courts as well as in politics) of those who believed that "injustices and inequities" were the causes of crime which marked a de-emphasis on law enforcement and imprisonment— and marked one of the most dramatic increases in crime in our history.

Having declined for decades on end, the murder rate suddenly doubled between 1961 and 1974. The rate at which citizens became victims of violent crimes in general tripled.

Such trends began at different times in different countries but the patterns remained very similar. As the rates of imprisonment declined, crime rates soared— whether in England, Australia, New Zealand or the United States.

After a whole generation of crime victims were sacrificed on the altar to the theories of the left, a political backlash produced higher rates of imprisonment— and lower rates of crime— in all these countries in the late 20th century.

We are still not back to where we were in 1960, as regards either the level of crime or the downward trend in murder rates. The notions of the left are still going strong in the media, in academia, and in politics.

The left is still comfortable talking about "injustices and inequities"— even without notes— and certainly without confronting the vast amount of evidence that they are wrong.

The Left and Crime: Part II

Do higher rates of imprisonment reduce crime? Is crime a result of poverty, unemployment, and the like? Are alternatives to incarceration more effective in preventing criminals from repeating their crimes?

Some people would hesitate to try to answer any of these questions before going through a lot of hard evidence and thinking it over very carefully.

But many on the left can answer immediately because they know what answers are already in vogue on the left— and that the only reason others don't accept those answers is because they are behind the times or just hard-hearted people who want to punish.

It is one thing to believe that policy *A* is better than policy *B*. It is something very different to believe that those who believe in policy *A* are wiser, more compassionate, and generally more worthy human beings than those who believe in policy *B*.

Turning the empirical question of the results of policy *A* versus the results of policy *B* into the more personal question of a wonderful Us versus a terrible Them makes it harder to retreat if the facts do not bear out the belief.

If the choice between policy *A* and policy *B* is regarded as a badge of personal merit, either morally or intellectually, then it is a devastating risk to one's sense of self to make empirical evidence the ultimate test.

Not only in the United States, but in other countries as well, the political left has held steadfastly to its assumptions and beliefs about crime for at least two centuries, not only in the absence of hard evidence but in defiance of two centuries' accumulation of evidence to the contrary, from countries around the world.

Where the dominance of the left is greatest— in the media and in academia, for example— facts to the contrary are seldom heard. The futility of imprisonment, for example, is a dogma on the left. It does no good to point out that crime rates in both Britain and the United States soared during the decade of the 1960s when poverty rates were going down— and imprisonment rates were also going down.

It does no good to point out that soaring crime rates in the United States began to turn down only after the declining rate of imprisonment was halted and reversed, leading to a rising prison population much deplored by liberals.

It does no good to point out that Singapore's imprisonment rate is more than double that of Canada— and its crime rate less than one-tenth the Canadian crime rate. Many in the West were appalled to discover some years ago, that an American first offender in Singapore was sentenced to corporal punishment.

Few of the indignant critics bothered to consider the possibility that this might be a way to prevent the young man from becoming a second offender— and perhaps saving him from a worse fate later on if he continued to disregard laws.

Self-defense against criminals is anathema to the left in both Britain and the United States, but in Britain the left has greater predominance. Britons who have caught burglars in their homes and held them at gunpoint until the police arrived have found themselves charged with a crime— even when it was only a toy gun.

Given the prevailing view in the British criminal justice system that burglary is a "minor" offense and the fierce hostility to guns, even toy guns, the homeowner is far more likely to end up behind bars than the burglar is.

The left's jihad against gun ownership by law-abiding citizens has produced a flood of distorted information. International comparisons almost invariably compare the United States with some country with stronger gun control laws and lower murder rates.

But, if facts really mattered, you could just as easily compare the United States to countries with stronger gun control laws and higher murder rates— Brazil and Russia, for example.

You could compare the United States with countries with more widespread gun ownership— Switzerland and Israel, for example— and lower murder rates. But that's only if facts are regarded as more important than the dogmas of the left.

Millions of crime victims pay the price of the left's illusions about crime— and about themselves.

High-Stakes Courts

Recent landmark court decisions are reminders that elections are not just about putting candidates in office for a few years. The judges that elected officials put on the bench can remake the legal landscape, change fundamental social policies and even affect the way wars are fought, long after those who appointed them have served their terms and passed from the scene.

The Supreme Court recently created a new "right" out of thin air for captured enemy soldiers and terrorists— the right to seek release in the federal courts, something that neither the Constitution nor the Geneva Convention provided.

The High Court has also struck down gun control laws as violations of the Second Amendment. Whatever the legal merits or the policy merits of that decision, it too is a major change, created by judges.

The point here is that federal judges, including Supreme Court justices, wield enormous— and growing— power. What that means is that when we vote for the candidates who will nominate and confirm judges, we are making decisions not only for ourselves but for generations yet unborn.

Recent momentous decisions of the U.S. Supreme Court have been decided by 5 to 4 votes, including the votes of justices appointed by presidents who are no longer living— Justice John Paul Stevens, appointed by President Ford, and Justice Anthony Kennedy, appointed by President Reagan.

Whoever is elected to the White House this November is expected to appoint two or three new members of the Supreme Court— justices who will be making major decisions affecting the future of American society, long after that president is gone.

Your children will be living during the lifetime tenure of those justices, and your grandchildren will be living in a world shaped by the precedents that those justices set.

In a year when dissatisfaction has been expressed by both Democrats and Republicans with the presidential candidates chosen by their own parties, it is worth keeping in mind the high stakes involved in judicial appointments— and therefore in presidential elections.

This is especially important to be kept in mind by voters who are thinking of venting their frustrations by voting for some third-party candidate that they know has no chance of being elected.

There will be a president chosen this November, and he will appoint Supreme Court justices during his term, regardless of whether you stay home or go to the polls.

His choices for the High Court will have a major impact on history, whether you vote after a sober consideration of many facts or vote on the basis of the candidate's rhetoric, style or demographics.

Even more important than the particular issues that courts will decide is the more fundamental issue of what a judge's role is in our system of Constitutional government.

In the gun control decision, for example, there were justices who read the history and meaning of the Second Amendment differently. What was most dangerous, however, was Justice Stephen Breyer's opinion that it was up to judges to weigh and "balance" the pros and cons of gun control laws.

If we have Constitutional rights only when judges like the end results, we may as well not have a Constitution.

Is the right to free speech to be put aside, and a journalist put behind bars, whenever a judge thinks that journalist went "too far" in expressing an opinion about some politician or bureaucrat? Is someone to be tried over again for the same crime, even after having been acquitted, if judges regard the Constitutional ban on double jeopardy as just a suggestion to be weighed and "balanced?"

We have already seen what happens when a 5 to 4 majority decides that politicians can seize your home and give it to somebody else, if judges don't think your property rights "balance" whatever politicians choose to call "the public interest."

When deciding which candidate you want in the White House for the next 4 years, it is worth considering what kind of judges you want on the federal courts for the next generation.

The Duke Rape Case

People who were not within 1,000 miles of Duke University have already taken sides in the case of a stripper who has accused Duke lacrosse players of rape. One TV talk show hostess went ballistic when a guest on her program raised questions about the stripper's version of what happened.

Apparently we dare not question accusations of rape when it involves the new sacred trinity of race, class, and gender.

Media irresponsibility is one thing. Irresponsibility by an agent of the law is something else— and much more dangerous. Prosecutors are not just supposed to prosecute. They are supposed to prosecute the right people in the right way. In this case, prosecutor Michael Nifong has proceeded in the wrong way.

Having an accuser or a witness pick out the accused from a lineup is standard procedure. That procedure not only serves to identify someone to be charged with a crime, it also tests the credibility of the accuser or witness— or it should, if the lineup is not stacked.

A lineup is supposed to include not only people suspected of a crime but also other people, so that it tests whether the accuser or witness can tell the difference, and is therefore credible. But the stripper who claimed to have been raped by members of the Duke lacrosse team was presented with a lineup consisting exclusively of photographs of members of the lacrosse team.

In other words, whoever she picked out had to be a lacrosse player and would be targeted, with no test whatever of her credibility, because there was no chance for her to pick out somebody who had no connection with the team or the university. Apparently District Attorney Nifong was no more willing to test the accuser's credibility than was the TV talk show hostess who went ballistic, though credibility is often crucial in rape cases.

Mr. Nifong went public with his having DNA evidence collected. Then, after the DNA failed to match that of the accused, the students were arrested anyway and their bail was set at $400,000— in a community where a youth accused of murder had bail set at $50,000.

When a prosecutor acts like he has made up his mind and doesn't want to be confused by the facts, that is when the spirit of the lynch mob has entered the legal system. When this happens on the eve of an election for the prosecutor, it looks even uglier.

If the young men accused of rape are in fact guilty, they need to be proved guilty because they are guilty, not because an election is coming up or there is racial hype in the media or a legally stacked deck. More important, we need to know that the rule of law is there for all of us, regardless of who we are or who our accuser might be.

Even beyond this case, we are increasingly becoming a society in which some people are allowed to impose high costs on other people at little or no cost to themselves. This sets the stage for extortion, not only of money but also of legal plea-bargains extorted by ambitious prosecutors.

The stripper, for example, does not even pay the price of having her name known, while the names and pictures of the accused young men are all over the media. Even if they are acquitted, or the charges thrown out of court, this case will follow them and they will be under a cloud for the rest of their lives.

Mr. Nifong has said that he has a third person whom he may indict. If so, he has already demonstrated to that third person what he can do by disgracing the other two and putting a heavy financial burden on their families for bail and lawyers. If that third person cannot stand the disgrace or his family cannot afford the expense, that is leverage for getting him to say whatever the prosecutor wants him to say.

This case presents opportunities as well as pressures. Race hustlers are having a field day, including the inevitable Jesse Jackson.

A fellow stripper who was at the same party sees in this an opportunity— in her own words— to "spin this to my advantage."

The biggest opportunity that this case presents is for District Attorney Michael Nifong to win his election, even if the case falls apart later and the law is cheapened by all this.

The Duke Rape Case: Part II

The worst thing said in the case involving rape charges against Duke University students was not said by either the prosecutor or the defense attorneys, or even by any of the accusers or the accused. It was said by a student at North Carolina Central University, a black institution attended by the stripper who made rape charges against Duke lacrosse players.

According to *Newsweek*, the young man at NCCU said that he wanted to see the Duke students prosecuted, "whether it happened or not. It would be justice for things that happened in the past."

This is the ugly attitude that is casting a cloud over this whole case. More important, this collective guilt and collective revenge attitude has for years been poisoning race relations in this country.

It has torn apart other countries around the world, from the Balkans to Sri Lanka to Rwanda. Nor is there any reason to think that the United States is exempt from such polarization.

At one time, the black civil rights leadership aimed at putting an end to racism, and especially to the perversion of the law to convict people because of their race, regardless of guilt or innocence.

Today, this young man at NCCU represents the culmination of a new racist trend promoted by current black "leaders" to make group entitlements paramount, including seeking group revenge rather than individual justice in courts of law.

This attitude poisoned the O.J. Simpson case and it is now polarizing reactions to the Duke University case. Racial polarization is a dangerous game, especially dangerous for minorities in the long run.

Tragically, the way the Duke case is being handled, it looks as if District Attorney Michael Nifong is pandering to these ugly feelings. Legal experts seem baffled as to why he is proceeding in the way that he is because it is hard to explain legally.

It is not hard to explain politically, however. The District Attorney may well owe his recent election victory to having tapped into the kinds of racial resentments expressed by the young man at North Carolina Central University.

Now Mr. Nifong is riding a tiger and cannot safely get off. His best bet may be to let this case drag on until it fizzles out, long after the media have lost interest. His extraordinary postponement of the trial for a year suggests that he understands that.

In the meantime, the taxi driver who provided the first airtight alibi for one of the accused Duke lacrosse players has been picked up by the police on a flimsy, three-year-old charge, supposedly about shoplifting. He was held for five hours for questioning— reportedly not about shoplifting, but about the Duke rape charges.

Does this smell to high heaven or what?

The taxi driver himself is not accused of shoplifting. But two women who were passengers in his cab were. Since when are taxi drivers held responsible for what their passengers did before or after being in their cab?

What purpose can this harassing of the taxi driver serve? His account of what happened in the Duke rape case has already been corroborated by a surveillance camera at the bank to which he took one of the lacrosse players, as well as by other time-stamped records indicating where his passenger was during the time when he was supposed to be raping a stripper.

If the prosecution cannot discredit the taxi driver's statement in a court of law, what can they gain by harassing him? One thing they can gain could be to at least stop the cabbie from going on television again to repeat what he has said before.

If nothing else, the harassment can serve as a warning to anybody else who might feel like coming forward with testimony that undermines the prosecution's case.

Is this America or some banana republic?

Some people in the media saw this case from day one as a matter of taking sides rather than seeking the truth. They want to be on the politically correct side— for a black woman against white men— and the facts be damned.

If such attitudes prevail, we will indeed become a banana republic. Or worse.

The Duke Rape Case: Part III

In the wake of recent bombshell revelations in the Duke University "rape" case, even some of District Attorney Michael Nifong's supporters have started backing away from him.

It was not just that the head of a DNA laboratory testified under oath in December that he and Nifong both knew back in April that there was no DNA from any of the Duke University lacrosse players found on the body of the stripper who accused them of rape— or even that the DNA of other men was found in her underwear and in intimate areas of her body.

What was really damning was that he and Nifong had agreed to keep this fact secret, despite requirements that exculpatory evidence be turned over to the defense. Moreover, last May District Attorney Nifong filed a statement saying that the prosecution "is not aware of any additional material or information which may be exculpatory in nature."

But he already knew what the DNA evidence was before he signed that statement.

The leading newspaper in town, which had supported Nifong in its editorials before these new revelations, now called his actions "flawed" and "inexplicable."

Nifong's actions are inexplicable only if you assume that his purpose was to get at the truth about what actually happened at the party where the stripper claimed to have been raped.

That assumption has never been made in this column. From day one, I have never believed that this case was about rape, about the Duke lacrosse players or about the "exotic dancers" or strippers.

District Attorney Nifong's actions are perfectly consistent and logical from start to finish, once you see that this case is about Nifong's own career.

Let us go back to square one. Where was Nifong before this case came along?

He had worked in the District Attorney's office for years and was appointed interim District Attorney himself only after the previous District Attorney left to become a judge. Now Nifong faced a tough election against a woman he had once fired and who would undoubtedly fire him if she became District Attorney.

Where would that leave Nifong? Out on the street at an age when most people are not likely to be starting a new career. His pension as well as his job could be in jeopardy. Moreover, his opponent was favored to win the election.

Then along came the Duke University "rape" case, like a deliverance from heaven.

Politically, the case had everything: white jocks from affluent families at a rich and prestigious university versus a black woman who was a student at a far poorer and less distinguished black institution nearby.

Above all, there were black voters who could swing the election Nifong's way if he played the race card and conjured up all the racial injustices of the past, which he would now vow to fight against in the present.

Who cared whose DNA was where? This case could save Nifong's career. There was nothing "inexplicable" about what he did. Despicable yes, inexplicable no.

His inflammatory outbursts against the Duke students in the media are not inexplicable. Neither was his failure to follow standard procedures in presenting the accuser with a lineup that included only white Duke lacrosse players.

The standard procedure of including in a lineup people who are not suspects in the case is intended to test the accuser's credibility. But why would he risk having the accuser's credibility tested before his election?

It was not a question of winning the case. It was a question of winning the election. As for the case, that was not scheduled to come to trial until a year later.

If you cared about justice, you would want to go to trial much sooner, either to nail the Duke students if they were guilty or exonerate them if they were not. But nothing suggests that this was Nifong's agenda.

Now that so many of his misdeeds have been so widely publicized, Nifong's agenda has to include keeping his job and avoiding disbarment, or even being prosecuted himself.

The Duke Rape Case: Part IV

Just before the Attorney General of North Carolina appeared on television to announce his decision on the Duke University "rape" case, one of the many expert TV legal commentators said that Attorney General Roy Cooper would probably use the words "insufficient evidence" but not the word "innocent" in dismissing the case.

As it turned out, the Attorney General did use the word "innocent," saying that he and his staff considered the accused students innocent. It was the only decent thing to do.

Anything less would have let the ugly accusation follow them for life and, years from now, when all the details of this sordid story have long since been forgotten, hang over their heads with a suspicion that they got off on some legal technicality.

What a difference a year makes. A year ago, there was a lynch mob atmosphere against the accused students— from the Duke University campus to the national media, and including the local NAACP and the ever-present Jesse Jackson.

These were affluent white male students and a poor black woman accusing them of rape. For those steeped in the new sacred trinity of "race, class, and gender," what more did you need to know, in order to know which side to come out on?

Duke University suspended the students when charges were filed, cancelled the entire remaining schedule of the lacrosse team for which they played, and got rid of the coach. Former Princeton University president William Bowen— a critic of college athletics— and the head of the local NAACP were called in to issue a report, which complained that Duke had not acted fast enough.

Meanwhile, 88 members of the Duke faculty took out an ad in the campus newspaper denouncing racism.

Among other things, the ad said, "what is apparent everyday now is the anger and fear of many students who know themselves to be objects of racism and sexism."

As for the demonstrations and threats loudly voiced by some local blacks, in the wake of the accusations against the Duke lacrosse students, the ad said:

"We're turning up the volume in a moment when the most vulnerable among us are being asked to quiet down while we wait. To the students speaking individually and to the protesters making collective noise, thank you for not waiting and for making yourself heard."

This year, after all the charges have collapsed like a house of cards, the campus lynch mob— including Duke University president Richard H. Brodhead— are backpedalling swiftly and washing their hands like Pontius Pilate.

They deny ever saying that the students were guilty. Of course not. They merely acted as if that was a foregone conclusion, while leaving themselves an escape hatch.

It is bad enough to be part of a lynch mob. It is worse to deny that you are part of a lynch mob, while standing there holding the rope in your hands.

What is even more important than clearing the names of the three young men charged with a heinous crime is making sure that the man responsible for this travesty of justice— District Attorney Michael Nifong— pays the fullest price for what he did.

The state bar association investigating Nifong needs to understand that this case is much bigger than Nifong.

If prosecutors can drag people through the mud and keep felony charges hanging over their heads, long after all the evidence contradicts the charges against them, then any of us, anywhere, can be put through a living hell whenever it suits the whim or the political agenda of a district attorney.

Much was made of the fact that these Duke students came from affluent families. Lucky for them— and for all of us. Not everyone has an extra million dollars lying around to fight off false accusations. Their fight is our fight.

This case will send a message, one way or another, to prosecutors across the length and breadth of this country. Either you can get away with dragging people through hell without a speck of evidence— and in defiance of evidence— or you can't.

This case has already sent a message about the kinds of gutless lemmings on our academic campuses, including our most prestigious institutions.

Good Riddance

When Supreme Court Justices retire, there is usually some pious talk about their "service," especially when it has been a long "service." But the careers of all too many of these retiring jurists, including currently retiring Justice John Paul Stevens, have been an enormous disservice to this country.

Justice Stevens was on the High Court for 35 years— mores the pity, or the disgrace. Justice Stevens voted to sustain racial quotas, created "rights" out of thin air for terrorists, and took away Americans' rights to their own homes in the infamous *Kelo* decision of 2005.

The Constitution of the United States says that the government must pay "just compensation" for seizing a citizen's private property for "public use." In other words, if the government has to build a reservoir or bridge, and your property is in the way, they can take that property, provided that they pay you its value.

What has happened over the years, however, is that judges have eroded this protection and expanded the government's power— as they have in other issues. This trend reached its logical extreme in the Supreme Court case of *Kelo v. City of New London*. This case involved local government officials seizing homes and businesses— not for "public use" as the Constitution specified, but to turn this property over to other private parties, to build more upscale facilities that would bring in more tax revenues.

Justice John Paul Stevens wrote the Supreme Court opinion that expanded the Constitution's authorization of seizing private property for "public use" to seizing private property for a "public purpose." And who would define what a "public purpose" is? Basically, those who were doing the seizing. As Justice Stevens put it, the government authorities' assessment of a proper "public purpose" was entitled to "great respect" by the courts.

Let's go back to square one. Just who was this provision of the Constitution supposed to restrict? Answer: government officials. And to whom would Justice Stevens defer? Government officials! Why would those who wrote the Constitution waste good ink putting that protection in there, if not to protect citizens from the very government officials to whom Justice Stevens deferred?

John Paul Stevens is a classic example of what has been wrong with too many Republicans' appointments to the Supreme Court. The biggest argument in favor of nominating him was that he could be confirmed by the Senate without a fight.

Democratic presidents appoint judges who will push their political agenda from the federal bench, even if that requires stretching and twisting the Constitution to reach their goals.

Republicans too often appoint judges whose confirmation will not require a big fight with the Democrats. You can always avoid a fight by surrendering, and a whole wing of the Republican party has long ago mastered the art of preemptive surrender.

The net result has been a whole string of Republican Justices of the Supreme Court carrying out the Democrats' agenda, in disregard of the Constitution. John Paul Stevens has been just one.

There may have been some excuse for President Ford's picking such a man, in order to avoid a fight, at a time when he was an unelected President who came into office in the wake of Richard Nixon's resignation in disgrace after Watergate, creating lasting damage to the public's support of the Republicans.

But there was no such excuse for the elder President Bush to appoint David Souter, much less for President Eisenhower, with back-to-back landslide victories at the polls, to inflict William J. Brennan on the country.

In light of these justices' records, and in view of how long these justices remain on the court, nominating such people was close to criminal negligence.

If and when the Republicans return to power in Washington, we can only hope that they remember what got them suddenly and unceremoniously dumped out of power the last time. Basically, it was running as Republicans and then governing as if they were Democrats, running up big deficits, with lots of earmarks and interfering with the market.

But the most lasting damage to the country has been putting people like John Paul Stevens on the Supreme Court.

A Tangled Web

While the recent Supreme Court decision in the New Haven firefighters' case will be welcome news to those who don't think that a gross injustice is O.K. when those on the receiving end are white, the reasoning behind the 5 to 4 decision is a painful reminder that the law is still tangled in a web of assumptions, evasions and contradictions when it comes to racial issues.

Nor have these problems been clarified with the passage of time. On the contrary, the growing complexity and murkiness of civil rights law over the years recalls the painful saying: "Oh, what a tangled web we weave when first we practice to deceive."

The original Civil Rights Act of 1964 was very straightforward in forbidding discrimination. But, even before that Act was passed, there were already people demanding more than equality of treatment. Some wanted equality of end results, some wanted restitution for past wrongs, and some just wanted as much as they could get.

Opponents of the Civil Rights Act said that it would lead to racial quotas and reverse discrimination. Advocates of the Act not only denied this, they wrote the language of the law in a way designed to explicitly prevent such things. But judges, over the years, have "interpreted" the Civil Rights Act to mean what its opponents said it would mean, rather than what its advocates put into the plain language of the legislation.

A key notion that has created unending mischief, from its introduction by the Supreme Court in 1971 to the current firefighters' case, is that of "disparate impact." Any employment requirement that one racial or ethnic group meets far more often than another is said to have a "disparate impact" and is considered to be evidence of racial discrimination.

In other words, if group X doesn't pass a test nearly as often as group Y, then there is something wrong with the test, according to this reasoning or lack of reasoning. This implicitly assumes that there cannot be any great difference between the two groups in the skills, talents or efforts required.

That notion is the grand dogma of our time— an idea for which no evidence is asked or given, and an idea that no amount of contradictory evidence can change in the minds of the true believers, or in the rhetoric of ideologues and opportunists. Trying to reconcile that dogma with the principle of equal treatment for all has led courts into feats of higher metaphysics that the Medieval Scholastics could be proud of.

The dogma survives because it is politically useful, not because it has met any test of facts. Innumerable facts against it can be found around the world and down through history.

All sorts of groups in all sorts of countries have been demonstrably better than other groups at particular things, whether economic, intellectual, political or military. This fact is so blatant that only people with great cleverness can manage to deny the obvious. That cleverness is what creates the tangled web of confusion that has plagued civil rights cases for decades.

Does anybody seriously doubt that blacks usually play basketball better than whites? Does anybody seriously doubt that the leading cameras and lenses in the world have long been produced by Germans and Japanese? Or that Jews have been over-represented among the top performers in various intellectual fields?

Many groups whose performances have greatly outstripped the performances of others in a particular field have often been in no position to discriminate, even when the disparities have been far greater than those between blacks and whites in the United States.

In a number of countries, powerless minorities have so outperformed the dominant majority that group preferences and quotas have been instituted to favor the majority group that has otherwise been unable to compete. This has happened in Malaysia, Sri Lanka, Nigeria, and Fiji, among other places. Before World War II, quotas to benefit the majority were common in a number of European universities, where Jewish students outperformed others.

It is not stupidity, but ideology and politics, which allow the "disparate impact" dogma to create a tangled web of deception in even the highest levels of our legal system. The recent Supreme Court's decision in the New Haven firefighters' case was a rare example of sanity prevailing, even if only by a vote of 5 to 4.

Talking Points

One of the many signs of the degeneration of our times is how many serious, even life-and-death, issues are approached as talking points in a game of verbal fencing. Nothing illustrates this more than the fatuous, and even childish, controversy about "torturing" captured terrorists.

People's actions often make far more sense than their words. Most of the people who are talking lofty talk about how we mustn't descend to the level of our enemies would themselves behave very differently if presented with a comparable situation, instead of being presented with an opportunity to be morally one up with rhetoric.

What if it was your mother or your child who was tied up somewhere beside a ticking time bomb and you had captured a terrorist who knew where that was? Face it: What you would do to that terrorist to make him talk would make water-boarding look like a picnic.

You wouldn't care what the *New York Times* would say or what "world opinion" in the U.N. would say. You would save your loved one's life and tell those other people what they could do.

But if the United States behaves that way it is called "arrogance"— even by American citizens. Indeed, even by the American president.

There is a big difference between being ponderous and being serious. It is scary when the President of the United States is not being serious about matters of life and death, saying that there are "other ways" of getting information from terrorists.

Maybe this is a step up from the previous talking point that "torture" had not gotten any important information out of terrorists. Only after this had been shown to be a flat-out lie did Barack Obama shift his rhetoric to the lame assertion that unspecified "other ways" could have been used.

For a man whose whole life has been based on style rather than substance, on rhetoric rather than reality, perhaps nothing better could have been expected. But that the media and the public would have become so mesmerized by the Obama cult that they could not see through this to think of their own survival, or that of this nation, is truly a chilling thought.

When we look back at history, it is amazing what foolish and even childish things people said and did on the eve of a catastrophe about to consume them. In 1938, with Hitler preparing to unleash a war in which tens of millions of men, women and children would be slaughtered, the play that was the biggest hit on the Paris stage was a play about French and German reconciliation, and a French pacifist that year dedicated his book to Adolf Hitler.

When historians of the future look back on our era, what will they think of our time? Our media too squeamish to call murderous and sadistic terrorists anything worse than "militants" or "insurgents"? Our president going abroad to denigrate the country that elected him, pandering to feckless allies and outright enemies, and literally bowing to a foreign tyrant ruling a country from which most of the 9/11 terrorists came?

It is easy to make talking points about how Churchill did not torture German prisoners, even while London was being bombed. There was a very good reason for that: They were ordinary prisoners of war who were covered by the Geneva Convention and who didn't know anything that would keep London from being bombed.

Whatever the verbal fencing over the meaning of the word "torture," there is a fundamental difference between simply inflicting pain on innocent people for the sheer pleasure of it— which is what our terrorist enemies do— and getting life-saving information out of the terrorists by whatever means are necessary.

The left has long confused physical parallels with moral parallels. But when a criminal shoots at a policeman and the policeman shoots back, physical equivalence is not moral equivalence. And what American intelligence agents have done to captured terrorists is not even physical equivalence.

If we have reached the point where we cannot be bothered to think beyond rhetoric or to make moral distinctions, then we have reached the point where our own survival in an increasingly dangerous world of nuclear proliferation can no longer be taken for granted.

Gay "Marriage"

Now that a number of state courts have refused to redefine marriage to include same-sex unions, cries of "discrimination" are being heard.

The "equal protection of the laws" provided by the Constitution of the United States applies to people, not actions. Laws exist precisely in order to discriminate between different kinds of actions.

When the law permits automobiles to drive on highways but forbids bicycles from doing the same, that is not discrimination against people. A cyclist who gets off his bicycle and gets into a car can drive on the highway just like anyone else.

In a free society, vast numbers of things are neither forbidden nor facilitated. They are considered to be none of the law's business.

Homosexuals were on their strongest ground when they said that the law had no business interfering with relations between consenting adults. Now they want the law to put a seal of approval on their behavior.

But no one is entitled to anyone else's approval.

Why is marriage considered to be any of the law's business in the first place? Because the state asserts an interest in the outcomes of certain unions, separate from and independent of the interests of the parties themselves.

In the absence of the institution of marriage, the individuals could arrange their relationship whatever way they wanted to, making it temporary or permanent, and sharing their worldly belongings in whatever way they chose.

Marriage means that the government steps in, limiting or even prescribing various aspects of their relations with each other— and still more their relationship with whatever children may result from their union.

In other words, marriage imposes legal restrictions, taking away rights that individuals might otherwise have. Yet "gay marriage" advocates depict marriage as an expansion of rights to which they are entitled.

They argue against a "ban on gay marriage" but marriage has for centuries meant a union of a man and a woman. There is no gay marriage to ban.

Analogies with bans against interracial marriage are bogus. Race is not part of the definition of marriage. A ban on interracial marriage is a ban on the same actions otherwise permitted because of the race of the particular people involved. It is a discrimination against people, not actions.

Justice Oliver Wendell Holmes said that the life of the law has not been logic but experience. Vast numbers of laws have accumulated and evolved over the centuries, based on experience with male-female unions.

There is no reason why all those laws should be transferred willy-nilly to a different union, one with no inherent tendency to produce children nor the inherent asymmetries of relationships between people of different sexes.

Despite attempts to evade these asymmetries with such fashionable phrases as "a pregnant couple" or references to "spouses" rather than husbands and wives, these asymmetries take many forms and have many repercussions, which laws attempt to deal with on the basis of experience, rather than theories or rhetoric.

Wives, for example, typically invest in the family by restricting their own workforce participation, if only long enough to take care of small children. Studies show such differences still persisting in this liberated age, and even among women and men with postgraduate degrees from Harvard and Yale.

In the absence of marriage laws, a husband could dump his wife at will and she could lose decades of investment in their relationship. Marriage laws seek to recoup some of that investment for her through alimony when divorce occurs.

Those who think of women and men in the abstract consider it right that ex-husbands should be as entitled to alimony as ex-wives. But what are these ex-husbands being compensated for?

And why should any of this experience apply to same-sex unions, where there are not the same inherent asymmetries nor the same tendency to produce children?

Tabloid TV "Justice"

Whether Zacarias Moussaoui received the death penalty or life imprisonment was never a big issue for me. What was appalling, however, was the way the penalty phase of his trial was conducted.

First, there was the parade of witnesses, including former New York Mayor Rudolph Giuliani, testifying as to the horrifying consequences of the 9/11 terrorist attacks and the terrible pain of those whose loved ones were killed.

What was the point of all this? We already know that murder is a bad thing, big time, not only for the victims but also for those survivors who loved the victims and will carry the emotional scars for years.

That is why there are laws against murder on the books in the first place.

There was a time when murderers were hanged or electrocuted without any of these emotional tabloid TV scenes in the courtroom— and without years, or even decades, of delay while all sorts of legal hand-wringing and nit-picking goes on in the appellate courts.

With our courts often so overcrowded that criminals are out on bail, walking the streets and committing new crimes, while awaiting trial on old charges, do we have the luxury of using up court time emotionalizing the obvious?

Are sentences supposed to fit the crime or to depend on what kind of show is put on in the courtroom?

A rational case could have been made for either the death penalty or life imprisonment. My own preference would be for an automatic death sentence for members of international terrorist organizations.

Talk about "life imprisonment without the possibility of parole" is misleading. There is no such thing as life imprisonment without the possibility of a liberal president being elected and issuing a pardon or an amnesty.

There is no such thing as life imprisonment without the possibility of escape— or of killing a fellow prisoner or a guard. For members of international terrorist networks, there is no such thing as life imprisonment without the possibility of fellow terrorists taking dozens of hostages and killing them if their guy is not set free.

The actual legal basis for the death penalty in the case of Zacarias Moussaoui was that he failed to tell authorities about the impending 9/11 attacks— and thereby contributed to the death of the thousands of victims of that attack.

If we want to repeal the Fifth Amendment against self-incrimination, then let's talk about that. But so long as the Fifth Amendment is part of the Constitution, a failure to tell all hardly seems like a basis for a death penalty.

None of this, however, seems to have been the real reason for not imposing the death penalty on Zacarias Moussaoui. Among the reasons apparently taken into consideration, according to the *New York Times*, was "his troubled upbringing in a dysfunctional immigrant Moroccan family in France."

Are only people with blissful childhoods to be held fully accountable for their crimes? Do jurors have any way of knowing how many other people with unhappy childhoods never murdered anybody?

Even if we take a completely deterministic view of crimes— that they are all due to circumstances beyond the individual's control— why should that lead to lesser punishments?

One of the factors we can control is punishment. But nothing a jury can do will stop people from having unhappy childhoods.

For centuries, we have quarantined innocent people who had some deadly dangerous and communicable disease through no fault of their own. Only in the case of AIDS did we stop doing this because of the political clout of the homosexual lobby.

The point here is that the safety of society usually overrides questions about some cosmic sense of justice for the individual. Jurors cannot act as if they were God on Judgment Day taking all individual circumstances into account. They are not equipped to do that and there is no point pretending that they are.

What people are equipped to do is show common sense. That is what our legal system is increasingly failing to do.

RANDOM THOUGHTS

From time to time, I run columns consisting solely of random thoughts on the passing scene. These columns seem to be especially popular with people who like my columns in general— and especially unpopular with critics. Because most of these columns contain some references to events that were topical at the time but are not any longer, these columns will not be reproduced here. Instead, individual selections from these columns will be presented.

R andom Thoughts on the Passing Scene:

Some people seem to think that we live in more "liberated" times, when all that has happened is that one set of taboos has been replaced by another and more intolerantly enforced set of taboos.

We all enter the world knowing nothing but, by the time we are teenagers, we know it all. Sometimes it is decades later before we know enough to realize how little we know.

One of the scariest aspects of our times is how easy it is for glib loudmouths to turn us against each other, weakening the whole framework of society, on which we all depend.

The adage "follow the money" will be hard to apply in the current administration, when there is so much money going in all directions that it is doubtful whether anybody can follow it.

It is amazing to me that there are people who still take seriously claims by some politicians that they are against "special interests." All politicians are against their opponents' special interests and in favor of their own special interests— which, of course, they don't call special interests.

Ronald Reagan had a vision of America. Barack Obama has a vision of Barack Obama.

You may scoff at the Tooth Fairy if you like. But the Tooth Fairy's approach has gotten more politicians elected than any economist's analysis has.

Stepping beyond your competence can be like stepping off a cliff. Too many people with brilliance and talent within some field do not realize how ignorant— or, worse yet, misinformed— they are when talking like philosopher-kings about other things.

If politicians stopped meddling with things they don't understand, there would be a more drastic reduction in the size of government than anyone in either party advocates.

Some people are so busy being clever that they don't have time enough to be wise.

Since this is an era when many people are concerned about "fairness" and "social justice," what is your "fair share" of what someone else has worked for?

Many colleges claim that they develop "leaders." All too often, that means turning out graduates who cannot feel fulfilled unless they are telling other people what to do. There are already too many people like that, and they are a menace to everyone else's freedom.

Despite people who speak glibly about "earlier and simpler times," all that makes earlier times seem simpler is our ignorance of their complexities.

Can you cite one speck of hard evidence of the benefits of "diversity" that we have heard gushed about for years? Evidence of its harm can be seen— written in blood— from Iraq to India, from Serbia to Sudan, from Fiji to the Philippines. It is scary how easily so many people can be brainwashed by sheer repetition of a word.

The reason so many people misunderstand so many issues is not that these issues are so complex, but that people do not want a factual or analytical explanation that leaves them emotionally unsatisfied. They want villains to hate and heroes to cheer— and they don't want explanations that fail to give them that.

For university presidents, as for politicians at all levels, one of the most valuable talents for the success of their careers is the ability to say things that make no sense, with a straight face and in a lofty tone.

Government bailouts are like potato chips: You can't stop with just one.

One of the ways in which people are similar is in the lengths to which they will go in order to show that they are different.

Doing 90 percent of what is required is one of the biggest wastes, because you have nothing to show for all your efforts. But doing 110 percent of what is expected is one of the smartest investments because it can pay off with a big reputation for just a little more effort.

A public opinion poll back in 1964 asked if America was worth fighting for— and 87 percent of blacks said "yes." Today, it is doubtful if any segment of the population would give that answer that often.

I have never seen a skinny cook.

"We are a nation of immigrants," we are constantly reminded. We are also a nation of people with ten fingers and ten toes. Does that mean that anyone who has ten fingers and ten toes should be welcomed and given American citizenship?

Sometimes we seem like people on a pleasure boat drifting down the Niagara river, unaware that there are waterfalls up ahead. I don't know what people think is going to happen when a nation that already sponsors international terrorism has nuclear bombs to give to terrorists around the world.

The beauty of doing nothing is that you can do it perfectly. Only when you do something is it almost impossible to do it without mistakes. Therefore people who are contributing nothing to society, except their constant criticisms, can feel both intellectually and morally superior.

"Global warming" seems to be joining "diversity," "gun control," "open space" and a growing list of other subjects where rational discussion has become impossible— and where you are considered a bad person even for wanting to discuss it rationally.

I have never understood stuttering. Once I heard a well-known economist, who stuttered, spend 45 minutes singing humorous, tongue-twister songs without a slip. Yet, after he finished— to rousing applause— he could barely get out the words "Thank you."

One of the signs of how easily we are bullied by small and vocal groups is how many universities, among other institutions, dare not even refer to the Christmas vacation but instead refer to "the winter holiday."

Who says that there is no difference between the political parties? When Democrats are criticized, they counter-attack. When Republicans are criticized, they whine that they are innocent.

I don't feel any different as I get older. However, I do notice that, when I am out biking, a lot of other bikers seem to be passing me and I don't seem to be passing anybody.

What is especially disturbing about the political left is that they seem to have no sense of the tragedy of the human condition. Instead, they tend to see the problems of the world as due to other people not being as wise or as noble as themselves.

We can only hope that the rumor that Israel is going to take out Iran's nuclear weapons facilities is true. If they do, Israel will be widely condemned by governments that are breathing a sigh of relief that they did.

Some of the biggest cases of mistaken identity are among intellectuals who have trouble remembering that they are not God.

I hate to hear about "partnerships" between government and business, or between government and other organizations. When there is a partnership between an ant and an elephant, who do you suppose makes the decisions?

There are too many people, especially among the intelligentsia, who will never appreciate the things that have made this country great until after those things have been destroyed— with their help. Then, of course, it will be too late.

We have now reached the truly dangerous point where we cannot even be warned about the lethal, fanatical and suicidal hatred of our society by Islamic extremists, because to do so would be politically incorrect and, in some European countries, would be a violation of the law against inciting hostility to groups.

Perhaps the scariest aspect of our times is how many people think in talking points, rather than in terms of real world consequences.

Liberals seem to think that they are doing lagging groups a favor by making excuses for counterproductive and self-destructive behavior. The poor do not need press agents. They need the truth. No one ever said, "Press agents shall make you free."

Socialists believe in government ownership of the means of production. Fascists believed in government control of privately owned businesses, which is much more the style of this government. That way, politicians can intervene whenever they feel like it and then, when their interventions turn out badly, summon executives from the private sector before Congress and denounce them on nationwide television.

Democrats could sell refrigerators to Eskimos before Republicans could sell them blankets.

A reader asks: "Why do we drive on the parkway and park on the driveway?"

I am so old that I can remember a Democrat, at his inauguration as President, say of our enemies: "We dare not tempt them with weakness."

In a democracy, we have always had to worry about the ignorance of the uneducated. Today we have to worry about the ignorance of people with college degrees.

I can't get as fiercely involved as some other people do in controversies about the origins of human life on earth. I wasn't there.

Does it tell you something about our times when a representative of the Taliban is welcome on the Yale University campus but representatives of our own military forces are not?

The political left loves to depict its ideas as "new"— a practice which is itself centuries old on the left, as are the ideas themselves.

When I think of the people with serious physical or mental handicaps who nevertheless work, I find it hard to sympathize with able-bodied men who stand on the streets and beg. Nor can I sympathize with those who give them money that subsidizes a parasitic lifestyle which allows such men to be a constant nuisance, or even a danger, to others.

If we each sat down and wrote out all the mistakes we have made in our lives, all the paper needed would require cutting down whole forests.

When you have 90 percent of what you want, think twice before insisting on the other 10 percent.

A sense of logic underlies a sense of humor. The same professor who wrote the first treatise on symbolic logic also wrote *Alice in Wonderland.*

Someone said that good judgment comes from experience— which in turn comes from bad judgment.

When I see people dealing lovingly with small children, it makes me feel that there may be hope for us, after all.

Climate statistics show that, with all the "global warming" hysteria today, our temperatures are still not as high as they were back in medieval times. Those medieval folks must have been driving a lot of cars and SUVs.

When my sister's children were teenagers, she told them that, if they got into trouble and ended up in jail, to remember that they had a right to make one phone call. She added: "Don't waste that call phoning me." We will never know whether they would have followed her advice, since none of them was ever in jail.

One of the painful signs of years of dumbed-down education is how many people are unable to make a coherent argument. They can vent their emotions, question other people's motives, make bold assertions, repeat slogans— anything except reason.

People who refuse to face the reality of hard choices are forever coming up with some clever "third way"— often leading to worse disasters than either of the hard choices.

Random Thoughts

Equal treatment of individuals does not mean equal treatment of behavior. That is why a polygamist is on the FBI's "most wanted" list. He is not allowed to redefine marriage to suit himself any more than the advocates of "gay marriage" are.

Since electricity is generated mostly by burning coal, has anyone calculated how much pollution is created by electric cars, even though none of that pollution comes out of their tailpipes?

Teaching is very easy if you don't care about doing it right and very hard if you do.

Now that the British television documentary, "The Great Global Warming Swindle" is available on DVD, will those schools that forced their students to watch Al Gore's movie, "An Inconvenient Truth" also show them the other side? Ask them.

Maybe the current bailout fever is Congress' way of getting into the spirit of the Yuletide season— saying in effect, "Yes, Virginia, there is a Santa Claus." They will undoubtedly also be saying, "Yes, New Jersey, there is a Santa Claus... Yes, Ohio, there is a Santa Claus. . ."

Wal-Mart has done more for poor people than any ten liberals, at least nine of whom are almost guaranteed to hate Wal-Mart.

If people had been as mealy-mouthed in centuries past as they are today, Ivan the Terrible would have been called Ivan the Inappropriate.

Will those who are dismantling this society from within or those who seek to destroy us from without be the first to achieve their goal? It is too close to call.